IoT Interview Han

101 Questions & Answers for Job Seekers

By

Sarful Hassan

Table of Contents

Preface

Welcome to the "IoT Interview Handbook: 101 Questions & Answers for Job Seekers." The world of the Internet of Things (IoT) is expanding rapidly, and skilled professionals are in high demand. This book is designed to help you prepare effectively for IoT interviews by covering a wide range of fundamental, technical, and real-world topics. Whether you're a beginner entering the industry or an experienced professional brushing up on your knowledge, this book will give you the confidence to succeed.

Who This Book Is For

This handbook is intended for:

- Job seekers preparing for IoT-related technical interviews

- Fresh graduates looking to break into the IoT industry

- Professionals seeking to switch careers into IoT

- Students and hobbyists who want to solidify their IoT knowledge base

How This Book Is Organized

The book is structured into five sections:

- Section 1: IoT Fundamentals

- Section 2: Hardware, Sensors & Devices

- Section 3: Networking & Protocols

- Section 4: Platforms, Cloud & Security

- Section 5: Real-World Scenarios & Projects

Each section builds progressively, offering a clear learning path from the basics to advanced concepts and practical project ideas.

What Was Left Out

This book focuses primarily on interview-relevant topics. In-depth coding projects, advanced research papers, and hardware schematics are beyond the scope but may be included in future editions.

Code Style (About the Code)

Where code snippets are mentioned (especially for microcontrollers or basic communication protocols), we follow a clean, beginner-friendly style using Arduino C, Python, or pseudocode for clarity. Real-world implementations may vary based on hardware and platform.

Release Notes

This is the first edition of the "IoT Interview Handbook." It reflects the current best practices and technologies up to early 2025. Future editions will expand based on industry trends and reader feedback.

Notes on the First Edition

All content has been curated carefully to be concise, practical, and immediately useful for interview preparation. We welcome suggestions for improvement!

MechatronicsLAB Online Learning

This book is part of the MechatronicsLAB learning series, dedicated to making technical education accessible, practical, and career-focused.

How to Contact Us

For feedback, questions, or collaborations:

- Email: mechatronicslab.net@gmail.com
- Website: mechatronicslab.net

Acknowledgments for the First Edition

A heartfelt thanks to everyone who contributed to the idea, structure, and fine-tuning of this handbook. Special thanks to the MechatronicsLAB community for continuous inspiration.

Copyright (MechatronicsLAB)

Disclaimer

This book is intended for educational purposes only. The author and publisher have made every effort to ensure the accuracy of the information. However, they assume no responsibility for errors, omissions, or damages resulting from the use of this information. Readers are encouraged to perform independent research and use professional judgment.

Section 1: IoT Fundamentals (1–25)

Interview Question 1: What Is the Internet of Things (IoT)?

Why This Question Is Asked: IoT is a rapidly growing field, and interviewers want to see if you understand its basics, real-world applications, and why it's important in modern technology.

What the Interviewer Wants to Know:

- Can you explain what IoT means in simple terms?
- Do you understand how devices are connected and communicate?
- Are you aware of real-world examples and its impact?

How to Structure Your Answer:

1. Define IoT in simple, clear terms
2. Mention how it connects devices and enables data exchange
3. Give examples of IoT applications

Sample Answer (Beginner): "The Internet of Things, or IoT, refers to a network of physical devices that are connected to the internet and can collect, share, and exchange data. These devices include everyday items like smartwatches, home security systems, and smart refrigerators. The goal of IoT is to make devices smarter and more useful by allowing them to communicate with each other and with users."

Sample Answer (Experienced): "IoT is the network of interconnected physical devices embedded with sensors, software, and other technologies to collect and exchange data over the internet. It enables automation, real-time monitoring, and smarter decision-making across industries such as healthcare, manufacturing, transportation, and smart homes. An example would be a smart thermostat that adjusts heating based on user behavior and weather predictions."

Beginner Tip: Focus on the idea that IoT makes everyday objects 'smart' by connecting them to the internet to gather, send, and act on data.

Final Thought: A strong understanding of IoT shows that you're familiar with one of the most transformative technologies shaping modern life, industries, and innovation.

Interview Question 2: What Are the Key Components of an IoT System?

Why This Question Is Asked: Understanding the core components of an IoT system shows that you grasp how these systems work together to collect, process, and act on data.

What the Interviewer Wants to Know:

- Can you identify the essential parts of an IoT system?
- Do you understand the role of each component?
- Can you explain how these components interact?

How to Structure Your Answer:

1. List the main components
2. Briefly explain the function of each
3. Mention how they interact to create a full system

Sample Answer (Beginner): "The key components of an IoT system include:

- **Devices/Sensors**: These gather data from the environment.
- **Connectivity**: This allows devices to send data to other devices or to the cloud, using Wi-Fi, Bluetooth, LTE, etc.
- **Data Processing**: Software processes the collected data, often in the cloud.
- **User Interface**: This lets users monitor and control devices, like through a smartphone app. All these parts work together to gather, transmit, analyze, and display information."

Sample Answer (Experienced): "An IoT system typically consists of:

- **Devices and Sensors**: They collect real-world data (e.g., temperature, location).
- **Connectivity Layer**: Communication networks (like MQTT, HTTP, Zigbee) transmit data.
- **Data Processing Layer**: Cloud platforms or edge computing solutions analyze and make sense of data.
- **Application Layer/User Interface**: Dashboards and control applications present the processed data to users and allow interaction. Each layer must work seamlessly to deliver real-time insights and automation, critical in industries such as healthcare, manufacturing, and smart cities."

Beginner Tip: Remember: Sensors collect data, connectivity sends it, processing analyzes it, and the interface lets users act on it.

Final Thought: A clear understanding of IoT system components highlights your ability to design or troubleshoot complete IoT solutions.

Interview Question 3: What Are the Major Applications of IoT?

Why This Question Is Asked: Interviewers want to check if you understand how IoT is applied across different sectors and how it transforms industries and everyday life.

What the Interviewer Wants to Know:

- Can you name key fields where IoT is being used?
- Do you understand how IoT brings value to these fields?
- Can you provide relevant real-world examples?

How to Structure Your Answer:

1. List major areas where IoT is applied
2. Give a short description of its role in each area
3. Mention specific examples if possible

Sample Answer (Beginner): "IoT is used in many fields. Some major applications include:

- **Smart Homes**: Devices like smart thermostats, lights, and security systems make homes more convenient and energy-efficient.
- **Healthcare**: Wearable devices monitor health conditions and share data with doctors.
- **Industrial Automation**: IoT sensors monitor machinery to improve efficiency and prevent breakdowns.
- **Agriculture**: Smart farming tools monitor soil conditions, weather, and crop health.
- **Transportation**: GPS trackers and smart traffic management systems optimize routes and safety. Each of these applications helps improve efficiency, safety, and convenience."

Sample Answer (Experienced): "IoT has transformed various industries, including:

- **Smart Homes and Buildings**: Enabling automation of lighting, climate control, and security.
- **Healthcare (IoMT)**: Remote patient monitoring, smart medical devices, and telemedicine platforms.
- **Industrial IoT (IIoT)**: Predictive maintenance, real-time production monitoring, and supply chain optimization.
- **Smart Cities**: Intelligent traffic systems, waste management, and public safety solutions.
- **Agriculture**: Precision farming through smart irrigation and crop monitoring.
- **Energy**: Smart grids and energy-efficient systems for homes and industries. These applications significantly boost efficiency, reduce costs, and enhance quality of life."

Beginner Tip: Link IoT to real-world improvements in comfort, health, productivity, and sustainability.

Final Thought: Knowing IoT applications shows that you see the practical impact of technology on modern society and business.

Interview Question 4: Explain the Difference Between IoT and M2M

Why This Question Is Asked: Interviewers want to check if you understand the subtle but important differences between Internet of Things (IoT) and Machine-to-Machine (M2M) communication.

What the Interviewer Wants to Know:

- Can you clearly define IoT and M2M?
- Do you understand how their scope, connectivity, and applications differ?
- Can you give examples to highlight the differences?

How to Structure Your Answer:

1. Define M2M and IoT separately
2. Highlight key differences (scope, connectivity, purpose)
3. Give simple real-world examples

Sample Answer (Beginner): "M2M, or Machine-to-Machine, is the direct communication between two devices without human involvement, like a vending machine sending stock updates to a server. IoT, or Internet of Things, is a broader concept where many devices are connected to the internet, collecting and sharing data for analysis and smarter decision-making. While M2M usually focuses on point-to-point communication, IoT involves large networks, cloud computing, and user interaction."

Sample Answer (Experienced): "M2M refers to technologies enabling direct communication between machines over wired or wireless networks, often used for monitoring and control (e.g., smart meters sending usage data to utility companies). IoT is a broader ecosystem where devices not only communicate but also integrate with cloud platforms, perform analytics, and enable user interaction through interfaces. In essence, M2M is typically a closed, point-to-point system, while IoT is an open, interconnected network providing value-added services through data analysis, automation, and intelligent decision-making."

Beginner Tip: Think of M2M as simple device-to-device communication, while IoT is about connected ecosystems involving people, data, and smarter operations.

Final Thought: Understanding the difference between M2M and IoT shows that you grasp the evolution of connectivity from isolated machine communication to a full, user-centric digital ecosystem.

Interview Question 5: What Is an IoT Ecosystem?

Why This Question Is Asked: Interviewers want to assess if you understand the full landscape of IoT beyond just devices—including networks, platforms, and stakeholders.

What the Interviewer Wants to Know:

- Can you define what an IoT ecosystem is?
- Do you know the different parts and players involved?
- Can you explain how everything integrates to create value?

How to Structure Your Answer:

1. Define an IoT ecosystem in simple terms
2. Describe the main components (devices, networks, platforms, users)
3. Mention examples of companies or services within an IoT ecosystem

Sample Answer (Beginner): "An IoT ecosystem is the complete network of devices, connectivity methods, cloud services, applications, and users that work together to make IoT solutions possible. It includes smart devices, communication networks, cloud platforms for processing data, and apps that users interact with. Companies like Amazon (Alexa devices) and Google (Nest products) have built strong IoT ecosystems."

Sample Answer (Experienced): "An IoT ecosystem is a dynamic, interconnected environment comprising hardware (sensors, actuators), communication protocols (Wi-Fi, 5G, Zigbee), cloud and edge computing platforms, data analytics tools, cybersecurity frameworks, and end-user applications. It involves multiple stakeholders such as device manufacturers, network providers, platform developers, and end-users, all collaborating to create integrated IoT solutions. Examples include smart home ecosystems, industrial IoT platforms, and connected healthcare networks."

Beginner Tip: Think of the IoT ecosystem as a "team" where every player (device, network, platform, user) has a role to make smart solutions work.

Final Thought: A strong grasp of the IoT ecosystem shows that you can think about IoT solutions holistically, considering both technical and user-centric aspects.

Interview Question 6: What Is Edge Computing?

Why This Question Is Asked: Interviewers want to assess if you understand modern computing trends, especially how edge computing fits into IoT and real-time data processing.

What the Interviewer Wants to Know:

- Can you explain edge computing in simple terms?
- Do you know why and when it is preferred over cloud computing?
- Can you mention examples where edge computing is useful?

How to Structure Your Answer:

1. Define edge computing clearly
2. Explain its advantages
3. Provide real-world examples

Sample Answer (Beginner): "Edge computing is when data is processed closer to where it is generated, like at the device itself, instead of sending it all the way to a cloud server. This helps to reduce delays, save bandwidth, and make quicker decisions. For example, a smart camera that analyzes video locally to detect motion instead of sending all footage to the cloud uses edge computing."

Sample Answer (Experienced): "Edge computing refers to the practice of processing data near the source of data generation rather than relying entirely on centralized cloud servers. It reduces latency, conserves bandwidth, and enables real-time insights, which are critical for applications like autonomous vehicles, industrial automation, and remote monitoring systems. By distributing computing tasks to the 'edge' of the network, systems can react faster and maintain higher reliability."

Beginner Tip: Focus on the idea that edge computing means "closer, faster, and smarter" data handling compared to cloud-only solutions.

Final Thought: Understanding edge computing is crucial because it is a key enabler for real-time, intelligent IoT systems and next-generation applications.

Interview Question 7: What Is Fog Computing?

Why This Question Is Asked: Interviewers ask this to check if you can differentiate between edge, fog, and cloud computing, and understand where fog computing fits in IoT architectures.

What the Interviewer Wants to Know:

- Can you define fog computing clearly?
- Do you know how it relates to edge and cloud computing?
- Can you give practical examples of its use?

How to Structure Your Answer:

1. Define fog computing
2. Explain its relationship with edge and cloud computing
3. Mention examples or scenarios where fog computing is applied

Sample Answer (Beginner): "Fog computing is like a middle layer between edge devices and the cloud. It processes data closer to where it's generated, but not directly on the device. Instead, the data is processed on a nearby local server or gateway. This reduces the need to send all data to the cloud and helps with faster responses. For example, a factory may use fog computing to quickly analyze machine data on local servers before sending important information to the cloud."

Sample Answer (Experienced): "Fog computing extends cloud computing to the edge of the network by placing compute, storage, and networking services closer to end devices. It acts as an intermediate layer, processing data locally at gateways or routers to reduce latency and bandwidth usage. Unlike edge computing, where processing happens directly on the device, fog computing processes data on nearby nodes before interacting with the cloud. It is commonly used in smart cities, industrial IoT, and connected vehicles to support real-time analytics and improve system resilience."

Beginner Tip: Imagine fog computing as "mini-clouds" close to devices, making decisions faster without sending everything to the distant cloud.

Final Thought: Knowing fog computing helps you understand how large IoT systems manage huge amounts of data efficiently without overwhelming cloud networks.

Interview Question 8: What Is Cloud Computing in the Context of IoT?

Why This Question Is Asked: Interviewers want to verify if you understand how cloud computing supports IoT systems by providing storage, processing power, and remote management capabilities.

What the Interviewer Wants to Know:

- Can you explain cloud computing clearly?
- Do you understand its role in handling IoT data?
- Can you provide examples of cloud-based IoT applications?

How to Structure Your Answer:

1. Define cloud computing simply
2. Describe its role in IoT systems
3. Provide examples where cloud computing supports IoT

Sample Answer (Beginner): "Cloud computing means using remote servers hosted on the internet to store, manage, and process data instead of doing it locally. In IoT, cloud computing collects data from connected devices, stores it, analyzes it, and sends back commands. For example, a fitness tracker sends your health data to a cloud server where you can view your performance through a mobile app."

Sample Answer (Experienced): "Cloud computing in IoT refers to utilizing scalable cloud infrastructure to store massive amounts of IoT data, perform complex analytics, and manage devices remotely. It provides a centralized platform where data from millions of devices can be aggregated, processed, and visualized. Services like AWS IoT Core, Microsoft Azure IoT Hub, and Google Cloud IoT offer device management, real-time data processing, and machine learning capabilities to enhance IoT solutions."

Beginner Tip: Think of cloud computing as the "brain" that helps IoT devices work together, process data, and become smarter.

Final Thought: Understanding cloud computing's role in IoT highlights your knowledge of how modern IoT systems achieve scalability, flexibility, and intelligence.

Interview Question 9: What Are Sensors and Actuators?

Why This Question Is Asked: Interviewers want to ensure you understand two fundamental components of IoT systems: how they sense the environment and how they interact with it.

What the Interviewer Wants to Know:

- Can you clearly define sensors and actuators?
- Do you understand their role in IoT systems?
- Can you give examples of each?

How to Structure Your Answer:

1. Define what a sensor is
2. Define what an actuator is
3. Provide examples of both

Sample Answer (Beginner): "Sensors are devices that detect and measure changes in the environment, like temperature, light, or motion, and convert them into data. For example, a temperature sensor in a smart thermostat measures room temperature. Actuators, on the other hand, take action based on commands, like turning on a fan or opening a valve. For example, a smart lock uses an actuator to lock or unlock a door remotely."

Sample Answer (Experienced): "Sensors are input devices that detect physical parameters such as temperature, pressure, light, humidity, or motion and convert them into electrical signals for data processing. Actuators are output devices that respond to control signals by performing actions, such as rotating a motor, opening a valve, or adjusting lighting levels. Together, sensors and actuators form the foundation of IoT systems by enabling environment monitoring and control."

Beginner Tip: Remember: Sensors "sense" and collect information; actuators "act" based on that information.

Final Thought: A good understanding of sensors and actuators shows that you know how IoT devices interact with the real world to automate and improve everyday processes.

Interview Question 10: What Is a Microcontroller and Its Role in IoT?

Why This Question Is Asked: Interviewers ask this to verify if you understand the central processing component that makes IoT devices "smart" and capable of decision-making.

What the Interviewer Wants to Know:

- Can you define what a microcontroller is?
- Do you understand how microcontrollers fit into IoT architectures?
- Can you give examples of their use in IoT applications?

How to Structure Your Answer:

1. Define what a microcontroller is
2. Explain its function within IoT devices
3. Provide real-world examples

Sample Answer (Beginner): "A microcontroller is a small computer on a single chip that includes a processor, memory, and input/output pins. It controls the operations of an IoT device, like reading data from sensors and sending commands to actuators. For example, an Arduino board in a smart irrigation system reads soil moisture data and turns on the water pump when needed."

Sample Answer (Experienced): "A microcontroller is an integrated circuit designed to perform specific operations by combining a CPU, memory, and input/output peripherals on a single chip. In IoT systems, microcontrollers act as the 'brains' of edge devices, handling sensor data collection, initial processing, decision-making, and communication with other devices or cloud platforms. Popular microcontrollers like the ESP32 or STM32 are widely used in applications such as smart homes, wearable devices, and industrial automation."

Beginner Tip: Think of a microcontroller as a tiny computer that makes IoT devices intelligent by controlling actions based on sensor inputs.

Final Thought: Understanding microcontrollers is crucial because they are the foundation that enables IoT devices to operate autonomously and interact with the physical and digital worlds.

Interview Question 11: What Are the Layers of IoT Architecture?

Why This Question Is Asked: Interviewers want to assess if you understand the structured approach to designing IoT systems and how data flows through various stages.

What the Interviewer Wants to Know:

- Can you name and explain the standard layers in IoT architecture?
- Do you understand the role of each layer?
- Can you describe how these layers work together?

How to Structure Your Answer:

1. List the typical layers
2. Briefly explain the function of each layer
3. Mention how data flows through them

Sample Answer (Beginner): "The main layers of IoT architecture are:

- **Perception Layer**: This layer includes sensors and devices that collect data from the environment.
- **Network Layer**: It transmits the collected data to other devices or to cloud servers.
- **Application Layer**: It provides services and applications to users, like smart home apps or health monitoring dashboards. These layers work together to sense, transmit, and use information effectively."

Sample Answer (Experienced): "The IoT architecture is typically structured into three major layers:

- **Perception Layer**: Responsible for physical sensing and identification. Devices like RFID tags, sensors, and cameras gather environmental data.
- **Network Layer**: Manages the transmission of data between perception devices and data processing centers via communication technologies such as Wi-Fi, LTE, or Zigbee.
- **Application Layer**: Provides end-user services, interfaces, and decision-making based on analyzed data, covering areas like smart cities, healthcare, and industrial automation. Some models also include Middleware and Business Layers for added complexity and management."

Beginner Tip: Remember: Perception = collect data, Network = move data, Application = use data.

Final Thought: Knowing the layers of IoT architecture shows that you understand the complete journey of data, from sensing the environment to delivering actionable insights to users.

Interview Question 12: What Is a Gateway in IoT?

Why This Question Is Asked: Interviewers want to check if you understand how gateways help IoT devices communicate effectively and securely with networks and cloud platforms.

What the Interviewer Wants to Know:

- Can you define an IoT gateway clearly?
- Do you understand its role in managing data and device communication?
- Can you give examples of how gateways are used?

How to Structure Your Answer:

1. Define what a gateway is
2. Explain its main functions
3. Provide real-world examples

Sample Answer (Beginner): "A gateway in IoT is a device that connects sensors and devices to the internet or cloud. It collects data from devices, processes it if needed, and sends it to cloud servers. It can also send commands back to devices. For example, a smart home hub acts as a gateway between your smart lights, locks, and the internet."

Sample Answer (Experienced): "An IoT gateway acts as a bridge between edge devices (sensors, actuators) and the cloud or central servers. It aggregates, filters, preprocesses, and secures data before transmitting it to cloud platforms. It often translates between different network protocols (e.g., Zigbee to Wi-Fi) and provides critical security functions such as encryption and authentication. Gateways are crucial in applications like industrial automation, smart agriculture, and smart cities."

Beginner Tip: Think of a gateway as a "translator and traffic manager" that ensures IoT devices talk to the cloud smoothly and safely.

Final Thought: Understanding the role of gateways is vital because they help scale IoT networks efficiently, enhance security, and optimize communication between devices and systems.

Interview Question 13: What Is the Role of Connectivity in IoT?

Why This Question Is Asked: Interviewers want to ensure you understand that without reliable connectivity, IoT systems cannot function effectively, as devices need to communicate and exchange data.

What the Interviewer Wants to Know:

- Can you explain why connectivity is essential in IoT?
- Do you know about different connectivity options?
- Can you describe how connectivity impacts performance?

How to Structure Your Answer:

1. Explain why connectivity is critical
2. Mention types of connectivity technologies
3. Describe its impact on IoT system performance

Sample Answer (Beginner): "Connectivity in IoT allows devices to send and receive data. Without it, devices would not be able to share information with other devices or with the cloud. Common types of connectivity include Wi-Fi, Bluetooth, cellular networks, and LPWAN. Good connectivity ensures that IoT devices work smoothly and provide real-time data."

Sample Answer (Experienced): "Connectivity serves as the communication backbone of IoT systems, enabling data transmission between devices, gateways, and cloud platforms. Different IoT use cases require specific connectivity technologies like Wi-Fi (local networks), LTE/5G (high-speed mobile networks), Zigbee (low-power mesh networks), and LPWAN (long-range, low-power communication). The choice of connectivity affects system scalability, latency, energy consumption, and reliability, making it a critical design consideration in IoT architecture."

Beginner Tip: Remember: No matter how smart a device is, without connectivity, it can't share its data or be remotely controlled.

Final Thought: A clear understanding of connectivity highlights your grasp of how IoT devices interact, collaborate, and deliver value in real-world applications.

Interview Question 14: Name Some Common IoT Communication Protocols

Why This Question Is Asked: Interviewers want to know if you are familiar with the different communication methods IoT devices use to exchange data reliably and efficiently.

What the Interviewer Wants to Know:

- Can you name important IoT communication protocols?
- Do you understand their basic purpose?
- Can you identify where each might be used?

How to Structure Your Answer:

1. List common protocols
2. Briefly explain their use
3. Mention examples of where they are applied

Sample Answer (Beginner): "Some common IoT communication protocols are:

- **Wi-Fi**: Used for home IoT devices like smart speakers and cameras.
- **Bluetooth**: Used for short-range communication, like fitness trackers.
- **Zigbee**: Used for low-power, short-range applications like smart lighting.
- **MQTT**: A lightweight messaging protocol ideal for sending data between devices and servers.
- **LoRaWAN**: Used for long-range, low-power applications like smart agriculture."

Sample Answer (Experienced): "Popular IoT communication protocols include:

- **Wi-Fi**: High-bandwidth, short-range communication, common in consumer IoT.
- **Bluetooth and BLE (Bluetooth Low Energy)**: Energy-efficient protocol for short-range device pairing and data exchange.
- **Zigbee and Z-Wave**: Mesh networking protocols used in smart home and building automation.
- **MQTT (Message Queuing Telemetry Transport)**: Lightweight publish-subscribe messaging protocol ideal for constrained devices.
- **CoAP (Constrained Application Protocol)**: A web transfer protocol optimized for simple devices.
- **LoRaWAN (Long Range Wide Area Network)**: Suitable for long-distance communication with minimal power consumption, ideal for agriculture, smart cities, and logistics."

Beginner Tip: Focus on remembering that different protocols are chosen based on range, power, and data needs.

Final Thought: Knowing IoT protocols shows that you understand how different devices "talk" to each other, which is crucial for designing and maintaining efficient IoT systems.

Interview Question 15: What Is MQTT?

Why This Question Is Asked: Interviewers want to see if you are familiar with MQTT, one of the most widely used lightweight communication protocols in IoT systems.

What the Interviewer Wants to Know:

- Can you define what MQTT is?
- Do you understand how it works?
- Can you explain why and where it is used?

How to Structure Your Answer:

1. Define MQTT simply
2. Describe how it works (publish/subscribe model)
3. Mention its benefits and typical use cases

Sample Answer (Beginner): "MQTT stands for Message Queuing Telemetry Transport. It is a lightweight messaging protocol used in IoT for sending small amounts of data over unreliable networks. It works with a publish/subscribe model where devices send messages to a broker and other devices can subscribe to receive those messages. It is commonly used in smart home devices, wearables, and remote sensors."

Sample Answer (Experienced): "MQTT (Message Queuing Telemetry Transport) is a lightweight, open-source messaging protocol designed for low-bandwidth, high-latency, or unreliable networks. It uses a publish/subscribe architecture where clients publish messages to topics, and subscribers receive updates on those topics through a centralized broker. MQTT is ideal for IoT systems because of its minimal overhead, efficient use of network resources, and support for Quality of Service (QoS) levels, making it highly reliable in constrained environments like remote monitoring, smart agriculture, and industrial automation."

Beginner Tip: Imagine MQTT like a post office: devices 'publish' letters (messages) to a box (broker), and other devices 'subscribe' to pick them up.

Final Thought: A good understanding of MQTT demonstrates your grasp of efficient IoT communication methods, essential for building reliable and scalable IoT systems.

Interview Question 16: What Is CoAP?

Why This Question Is Asked: Interviewers want to check if you understand alternative lightweight protocols like CoAP, which are important for constrained IoT environments.

What the Interviewer Wants to Know:

- Can you define what CoAP is?
- Do you understand how it is different from other protocols like HTTP?
- Can you explain where CoAP is used?

How to Structure Your Answer:

1. Define CoAP simply
2. Explain how it works (request/response model)
3. Mention its advantages and typical applications

Sample Answer (Beginner): "CoAP stands for Constrained Application Protocol. It is a lightweight protocol designed for simple devices that need to communicate over the internet. CoAP works like HTTP with request and response methods but uses less data and is better suited for small, low-power devices like smart sensors in home automation."

Sample Answer (Experienced): "CoAP (Constrained Application Protocol) is a specialized web transfer protocol optimized for constrained nodes and low-power, lossy networks. It follows a request/response model similar to HTTP but uses UDP instead of TCP, making it lightweight and faster. CoAP supports multicast communication, low overhead, and asynchronous message exchanges, making it ideal for smart lighting systems, environmental monitoring, and building automation where efficient, real-time communication is needed."

Beginner Tip: Think of CoAP as a "lighter" version of HTTP, perfect for tiny devices with limited power and network capabilities.

Final Thought: Understanding CoAP shows that you are aware of specialized communication strategies tailored for efficient IoT operations in resource-constrained environments.

Interview Question 17: What Is HTTP and How Is It Used in IoT?

Why This Question Is Asked: Interviewers want to see if you understand how traditional internet protocols like HTTP fit into IoT systems, even though they were not designed specifically for constrained environments.

What the Interviewer Wants to Know:

- Can you define HTTP?
- Do you understand how HTTP is adapted for IoT use?
- Can you give examples of HTTP usage in IoT applications?

How to Structure Your Answer:

1. Define HTTP simply
2. Explain how it is used in IoT
3. Mention advantages, limitations, and examples

Sample Answer (Beginner): "HTTP stands for HyperText Transfer Protocol. It is a common way for computers to send and receive data over the internet. In IoT, devices use HTTP to communicate with web servers or cloud services. For example, a smart thermostat might send temperature readings to a cloud server using HTTP. However, HTTP can be heavy for small IoT devices because it requires more bandwidth and power."

Sample Answer (Experienced): "HTTP (HyperText Transfer Protocol) is a client-server communication protocol based on a request/response model, traditionally used for web browsing. In IoT, HTTP is employed when devices need to interact with RESTful APIs, exchange data with cloud servers, or integrate into existing web-based systems. While HTTP is simple and widely supported, it is relatively heavy for constrained devices, often leading to the adoption of lighter alternatives like MQTT or CoAP. HTTP is common in smart appliances, home automation hubs, and basic IoT monitoring applications."

Beginner Tip: Think of HTTP as a "universal language" that IoT devices can use to talk to web servers, but it might not always be the best choice for very small, battery-powered devices.

Final Thought: Understanding HTTP in IoT contexts shows that you know how traditional internet technologies are adapted (and sometimes replaced) to suit the unique needs of connected devices.

Interview Question 18: What Is the Difference Between TCP and UDP?

Why This Question Is Asked: Interviewers want to assess your understanding of fundamental networking concepts, especially in the context of IoT communication where reliability, speed, and resource constraints are important factors.

What the Interviewer Wants to Know:

- Can you clearly differentiate between TCP and UDP?
- Do you understand when each protocol is preferable?
- Can you explain their relevance to IoT applications?

How to Structure Your Answer:

1. Define TCP and UDP separately
2. Highlight key differences (reliability, speed, overhead)
3. Mention use cases for each

Sample Answer (Beginner): "TCP (Transmission Control Protocol) is a reliable communication method where data is checked and rechecked to make sure it arrives correctly. UDP (User Datagram Protocol) is faster but less reliable because it doesn't guarantee that the data will reach its destination. In IoT, TCP might be used for applications like sending important commands, while UDP is used for real-time data like video streaming."

Sample Answer (Experienced): "TCP (Transmission Control Protocol) provides reliable, connection-oriented communication by establishing a session between sender and receiver, ensuring ordered and error-checked data delivery. UDP (User Datagram Protocol) offers connectionless, best-effort communication without guaranteeing message delivery or order, making it lightweight and faster. In IoT, TCP is used for critical applications requiring data integrity (e.g., firmware updates), while UDP is preferred for real-time, low-latency communication (e.g., sensor telemetry, video feeds)."

Beginner Tip: Remember: TCP is "safe but slower," UDP is "fast but risky."

Final Thought: Understanding TCP and UDP differences is vital for designing IoT systems that balance speed, reliability, and resource efficiency according to the needs of the application.

Interview Question 19: What Is Latency and How Does It Affect IoT?

Why This Question Is Asked: Interviewers want to check if you understand the importance of quick data transmission in IoT systems and how latency can impact device performance and user experience.

What the Interviewer Wants to Know:

- Can you define latency clearly?
- Do you understand how latency impacts IoT applications?
- Can you explain scenarios where low latency is critical?

How to Structure Your Answer:

1. Define latency simply
2. Explain why it matters in IoT
3. Provide examples of high and low latency scenarios

Sample Answer (Beginner): "Latency is the time delay between sending a command and receiving a response. In IoT, low latency is important when devices need to react quickly, like in smart cars or healthcare monitors. High latency could cause slow responses and problems in critical systems."

Sample Answer (Experienced): "Latency refers to the time it takes for data to travel from a source to a destination and back. In IoT systems, high latency can negatively impact real-time applications such as autonomous vehicles, industrial control systems, and healthcare monitoring where immediate actions are crucial. Low-latency communication ensures quick decision-making, seamless automation, and better user experiences. Techniques like edge computing and optimized network protocols are often used to reduce latency in IoT deployments."

Beginner Tip: Think of latency as the "waiting time" between asking a question and getting an answer from a device.

Final Thought: Understanding latency is crucial for designing IoT systems that need real-time responsiveness, especially in safety-critical and time-sensitive applications.

Interview Question 20: What Are Smart Devices?

Why This Question Is Asked: Interviewers want to see if you understand what makes a device "smart" and how these devices fit into the IoT ecosystem.

What the Interviewer Wants to Know:

- Can you define what smart devices are?
- Do you understand the features that make them 'smart'?
- Can you give real-world examples?

How to Structure Your Answer:

1. Define smart devices simply
2. Explain key features (connectivity, data processing, automation)
3. Mention examples of smart devices

Sample Answer (Beginner): "Smart devices are electronic devices that can connect to the internet or other networks to collect, share, and act on information. They often have sensors and can make decisions automatically or be controlled remotely. Examples include smart TVs, smart thermostats, and smartwatches."

Sample Answer (Experienced): "Smart devices are network-connected electronic devices embedded with sensors, processors, and communication interfaces, enabling them to collect data, analyze it, and make decisions or interact with users autonomously or semi-autonomously. They are key components of IoT ecosystems, supporting automation, remote control, and real-time data monitoring. Examples include smart refrigerators that track food inventory, smart security cameras with motion detection, and voice-activated smart speakers."

Beginner Tip: Think of a smart device as a "regular device + internet + intelligence."

Final Thought: Understanding smart devices is fundamental because they are the front line of IoT, interacting directly with users and the environment to deliver intelligent services.

Interview Question 21: How Does IoT Impact Industries (e.g., Healthcare, Agriculture)?

Why This Question Is Asked: Interviewers want to know if you understand the real-world value IoT brings to different industries by improving efficiency, safety, and decision-making.

What the Interviewer Wants to Know:

- Can you describe how IoT is used across different industries?
- Do you understand the specific benefits it brings?
- Can you provide examples of IoT-driven transformations?

How to Structure Your Answer:

1. Mention industries impacted by IoT
2. Explain the role IoT plays in each
3. Give examples to illustrate your points

Sample Answer (Beginner): "IoT is changing many industries. In healthcare, it helps doctors monitor patients remotely using smart devices like heart rate monitors. In agriculture, IoT sensors track soil moisture and weather to help farmers grow crops better. In factories, IoT helps machines run more efficiently and predict problems before they happen."

Sample Answer (Experienced): "IoT significantly impacts industries by enabling real-time monitoring, automation, and data-driven decision-making. In healthcare, IoT supports remote patient monitoring, smart medical devices, and improved patient care through continuous health data collection. In agriculture, IoT powers precision farming by monitoring soil conditions, weather patterns, and crop health to optimize resource use and increase yields. In manufacturing (Industrial IoT), predictive maintenance reduces downtime, and connected supply chains improve logistics efficiency. These advancements result in cost savings, increased productivity, and enhanced service delivery."

Beginner Tip: Think about how 'smart' devices and sensors help industries work faster, safer, and smarter.

Final Thought: Recognizing IoT's industry impact demonstrates your ability to see the bigger picture of how connected technologies drive innovation and efficiency in real-world applications.

Interview Question 22: What Is Digital Twin Technology?

Why This Question Is Asked: Interviewers want to assess if you understand one of the advanced concepts associated with IoT, which is crucial for simulation, monitoring, and optimization of real-world systems.

What the Interviewer Wants to Know:

- Can you define digital twin technology?
- Do you understand how it relates to IoT?
- Can you provide real-world examples of its use?

How to Structure Your Answer:

1. Define digital twin technology
2. Explain how it works alongside IoT
3. Mention practical applications

Sample Answer (Beginner): "A digital twin is a virtual copy of a real-world object or system. It uses data from sensors on the real thing to update the virtual version in real time. For example, a factory machine might have a digital twin that shows how it's working, helping engineers spot problems before they happen."

Sample Answer (Experienced): "Digital twin technology involves creating a dynamic virtual model of a physical asset, system, or process. By integrating real-time data from IoT sensors, the digital twin mirrors the state, behavior, and performance of the real-world entity. It is used for simulation, predictive maintenance, optimization, and decision-making. Applications include smart manufacturing (predicting machine failures), smart cities (simulating traffic patterns), and healthcare (modeling patient vitals for remote monitoring)."

Beginner Tip: Think of a digital twin as a "living, breathing" model of something physical, constantly updated with real-world data.

Final Thought: Understanding digital twin technology shows that you grasp how IoT moves beyond simple monitoring into advanced simulation and intelligent optimization.

Interview Question 23: What Is LPWAN?

Why This Question Is Asked: Interviewers want to test your knowledge of network technologies tailored for IoT devices that require long-range communication with low power consumption.

What the Interviewer Wants to Know:

- Can you define LPWAN clearly?
- Do you understand why LPWAN is important in IoT?
- Can you give examples of LPWAN technologies and their applications?

How to Structure Your Answer:

1. Define LPWAN simply
2. Explain its characteristics (long-range, low-power)
3. Provide examples and use cases

Sample Answer (Beginner): "LPWAN stands for Low-Power Wide-Area Network. It's a type of wireless network that lets devices send small amounts of data over long distances using very little power. It's often used in smart agriculture, smart cities, and environmental monitoring where devices need to work for years on a battery. Examples include LoRaWAN and Sigfox."

Sample Answer (Experienced): "LPWAN (Low-Power Wide-Area Network) is a category of wireless communication technologies designed to enable long-range communication at low bit rates between battery-powered devices. LPWAN solutions, such as LoRaWAN, Sigfox, and NB-IoT, are ideal for IoT applications requiring extended device life, wide-area coverage, and minimal data transmission, like smart metering, asset tracking, and remote environmental sensing. LPWAN protocols are critical for connecting devices in rural, urban, and industrial settings where conventional Wi-Fi or cellular networks are impractical."

Beginner Tip: Think of LPWAN as "talking from very far away without needing much battery."

Final Thought: Understanding LPWAN technologies shows that you know how IoT devices can stay connected efficiently even in remote or power-constrained environments.

Interview Question 24: What Are IoT Edge Devices?

Why This Question Is Asked: Interviewers want to assess if you understand what edge devices are, their role in processing data locally, and their importance in reducing latency and bandwidth usage in IoT systems.

What the Interviewer Wants to Know:

- Can you define IoT edge devices?
- Do you understand their role compared to cloud-based processing?
- Can you give examples of edge devices in action?

How to Structure Your Answer:

1. Define IoT edge devices simply
2. Explain their key functions (local data processing, reduced latency)
3. Provide examples of where they are used

Sample Answer (Beginner): "IoT edge devices are smart devices that can collect and process data close to where it is created instead of sending everything to the cloud. This makes things faster and saves internet bandwidth. Examples include smart security cameras that detect motion and industrial sensors that analyze machine health on-site."

Sample Answer (Experienced): "IoT edge devices are network-connected hardware components (such as sensors, actuators, gateways, and microcontrollers) that perform data collection, local processing, and initial analytics near the source of data generation. By processing data at the edge rather than sending everything to a centralized cloud, these devices enable low-latency decision-making, reduce bandwidth consumption, and improve system reliability. Examples include smart surveillance cameras with built-in facial recognition, industrial robots with predictive maintenance capabilities, and smart meters that preprocess energy usage data."

Beginner Tip: Think of edge devices as "mini-computers" that make quick decisions before sending important information to the cloud.

Final Thought: Understanding IoT edge devices shows that you grasp modern approaches to making IoT systems faster, more efficient, and more reliable by minimizing reliance on centralized cloud infrastructure.

Interview Question 25: What Are the Challenges in IoT Development?

Why This Question Is Asked: Interviewers want to see if you are aware of the real-world difficulties in building, deploying, and maintaining IoT systems beyond just the technical basics.

What the Interviewer Wants to Know:

- Can you identify major technical and operational challenges?
- Do you understand how these challenges impact IoT projects?
- Can you suggest ways to address or mitigate these challenges?

How to Structure Your Answer:

1. List common challenges
2. Briefly explain each challenge
3. Mention how they can be addressed

Sample Answer (Beginner): "IoT development faces challenges like:

- **Security**: Protecting devices and data from hackers.
- **Connectivity**: Keeping devices reliably connected over different networks.
- **Power Management**: Making sure battery-powered devices last a

long time.

- **Data Management**: Handling huge amounts of data collected by sensors.
- **Interoperability**: Making different devices and platforms work together. To solve these, developers use encryption, optimize network choices, and design energy-efficient devices."

Sample Answer (Experienced): "Key challenges in IoT development include:

- **Security and Privacy**: IoT devices are vulnerable to cyberattacks due to limited processing power and weak encryption.
- **Scalability**: Managing millions of devices and data streams efficiently.
- **Data Overload**: Extracting meaningful insights from massive unstructured data sets.
- **Connectivity and Network Management**: Ensuring reliable, cost-effective, and low-latency communication.
- **Device Interoperability**: Integrating heterogeneous devices across different manufacturers and standards.
- **Energy Constraints**: Designing low-power devices that can operate for years without battery replacement. Overcoming these requires robust encryption, edge computing, standardized protocols, scalable cloud infrastructure, and efficient device design."

Beginner Tip: Remember: Building an IoT system is not just about connecting devices—it's about making them secure, reliable, scalable, and efficient.

Final Thought: Understanding IoT challenges shows that you have a realistic and practical view of what it takes to deliver successful IoT solutions in the real world.

Section 2: Hardware, Sensors & Devices (26–50)

Interview Question 26: What Is a Microcontroller Unit (MCU)?

Why This Question Is Asked: Interviewers want to ensure you understand what an MCU is and its critical role in embedded systems and IoT devices.

What the Interviewer Wants to Know:

- Can you clearly define an MCU?
- Do you know what components it includes?
- Can you explain its importance in IoT and embedded applications?

How to Structure Your Answer:

1. Define what an MCU is
2. Mention its key components
3. Explain its role with examples

Sample Answer (Beginner): "An MCU, or Microcontroller Unit, is a small computer built into a single chip. It has a processor, memory, and input/output pins all in one package. MCUs are used to control other parts of a system. For example, a microcontroller inside a smart thermostat reads temperature sensors and adjusts the heating automatically."

Sample Answer (Experienced): "A Microcontroller Unit (MCU) is an integrated circuit designed to perform specific control tasks. It combines a CPU (Central Processing Unit), RAM (Random Access Memory), ROM/Flash memory, and various input/output (I/O) peripherals like ADCs, timers, and communication interfaces (UART, SPI, I2C) on a single chip. MCUs are the 'brains' of embedded and IoT systems, handling real-time data processing and control tasks in applications such as home automation, industrial machinery, and wearable devices. Popular examples include ARM Cortex-M series, AVR microcontrollers, and ESP32."

Beginner Tip: Think of an MCU as a "tiny computer" that controls smart devices by processing sensor data and sending commands to actuators.

Final Thought: Understanding what an MCU is shows that you know the foundational hardware enabling intelligent, connected devices in embedded and IoT ecosystems.

Interview Question 27: Name Some Popular Microcontrollers Used in IoT Projects

Why This Question Is Asked: Interviewers want to see if you are familiar with common hardware platforms used in real-world IoT development.

What the Interviewer Wants to Know:

- Can you list widely-used MCUs in IoT?
- Do you understand why they are chosen?
- Can you mention a few use cases?

How to Structure Your Answer:

1. List several popular microcontrollers
2. Briefly describe why they are used
3. Provide examples of typical applications

Sample Answer (Beginner): "Some popular microcontrollers for IoT projects are:

- **Arduino Uno**: Easy for beginners, used in simple home automation projects.
- **ESP8266**: Built-in Wi-Fi, good for smart home devices.
- **ESP32**: Dual-core processor, Bluetooth and Wi-Fi support, used in wearable tech.
- **Raspberry Pi Pico**: Affordable and flexible for hobbyist IoT projects. These MCUs are chosen because they are cheap, powerful, and have good community support."

Sample Answer (Experienced): "Widely used microcontrollers in IoT include:

- **ESP32**: Dual-core, integrated Wi-Fi and Bluetooth, ideal for complex IoT solutions.
- **ESP8266**: Cost-effective Wi-Fi-enabled MCU used in smart home and DIY projects.
- **Arduino Uno (ATmega328P)**: Popular for rapid prototyping and educational purposes.
- **STM32 Series**: ARM Cortex-M-based MCUs used in industrial and medical IoT applications.
- **Raspberry Pi Pico (RP2040)**: Versatile dual-core MCU with strong I/O capabilities for low-power IoT devices. These MCUs are favored for their balance of performance, power efficiency, connectivity options, and developer ecosystem."

Beginner Tip: Focus on remembering ESP32 and Arduino Uno—they are among the most common and beginner-friendly MCUs.

Final Thought: Knowing popular microcontrollers shows that you are familiar with the essential hardware building blocks of IoT systems and capable of choosing the right platform for different projects.

Interview Question 28: What Is an SoC (System on Chip)?

Why This Question Is Asked: Interviewers want to assess if you understand the concept of hardware integration and how SoCs are essential for compact, power-efficient IoT designs.

What the Interviewer Wants to Know:

- Can you define what an SoC is?
- Do you understand its components and benefits?
- Can you mention examples and real-world applications?

How to Structure Your Answer:

1. Define SoC simply
2. Explain its components (CPU, memory, interfaces)
3. Mention examples and use cases

Sample Answer (Beginner): "An SoC, or System on Chip, is a tiny computer where everything—processor, memory, and other parts—is built into one single chip. It saves space and power, making it perfect for smartphones, smartwatches, and IoT devices like smart sensors."

Sample Answer (Experienced): "A System on Chip (SoC) integrates all major components of a computer—CPU, memory, input/output ports, storage controllers, and communication interfaces—onto a single silicon chip. SoCs offer high performance, energy efficiency, and compactness, making them ideal for space-constrained and battery-powered IoT applications. Examples include the ESP32 (IoT), Apple's A-series chips (smartphones), and Qualcomm Snapdragon SoCs. In IoT, SoCs power smart home devices, wearable tech, and edge processing nodes."

Beginner Tip: Think of an SoC as a "full computer shrunk down to fit on a small chip."

Final Thought: Understanding SoCs is important because they are the hardware backbone of many compact, efficient, and intelligent IoT and mobile devices.

Interview Question 29: What Are Analog and Digital Sensors?

Why This Question Is Asked: Interviewers want to check if you understand the basic types of sensors and how they produce different kinds of outputs that affect IoT system design.

What the Interviewer Wants to Know:

- Can you clearly differentiate between analog and digital sensors?
- Do you understand their output types and where they are used?
- Can you give examples of each?

How to Structure Your Answer:

1. Define analog and digital sensors separately
2. Explain the differences in their outputs
3. Provide examples and use cases

Sample Answer (Beginner): "Analog sensors create continuous signals that can have any value within a range. A good example is a temperature sensor that changes voltage smoothly with temperature. Digital sensors give specific values, usually just 0s and 1s. For example, a digital temperature sensor sends exact numbers like 25°C directly to a microcontroller."

Sample Answer (Experienced): "Analog sensors produce continuous output signals (like voltage or current) proportional to the physical parameter being measured, requiring analog-to-digital conversion for processing. Examples include LM35 temperature sensors and LDRs (light-dependent resistors). Digital sensors, on the other hand, generate discrete digital signals, often using built-in ADCs (Analog-to-Digital Converters) to output binary or encoded data. Examples include DHT11 humidity sensors and DS18B20 digital temperature sensors. Digital sensors offer easier integration with microcontrollers and more noise-resilient communication."

Beginner Tip: Remember: Analog = smooth, continuous signals; Digital = exact, step-by-step signals.

Final Thought: Understanding analog and digital sensors is crucial because it influences how you design circuits, choose microcontrollers, and process sensor data in IoT and embedded systems.

Interview Question 30: Name Common Sensors Used in IoT

Why This Question Is Asked: Interviewers want to ensure you are familiar with widely used sensor types in IoT projects and understand their real-world applications.

What the Interviewer Wants to Know:

- Can you list important sensors used in IoT?
- Do you know what each sensor measures?
- Can you mention typical use cases?

How to Structure Your Answer:

1. List several common IoT sensors
2. Briefly mention what they measure
3. Provide example applications

Sample Answer (Beginner): "Some common IoT sensors are:

- **Temperature Sensors**: Measure temperature (e.g., DS18B20 in smart thermostats).
- **Humidity Sensors**: Measure air moisture (e.g., DHT22 in weather stations).
- **Motion Sensors**: Detect movement (e.g., PIR sensors in smart lights).
- **Light Sensors**: Measure light levels (e.g., LDR in smart streetlights).
- **Gas Sensors**: Detect gases like CO_2 (e.g., MQ-2 in air quality monitors). These sensors help devices collect important environmental data."

Sample Answer (Experienced): "Common sensors used in IoT applications include:

- **Temperature Sensors (e.g., LM35, DS18B20):** Monitor environmental or device temperatures.
- **Humidity Sensors (e.g., DHT11, DHT22):** Measure atmospheric humidity for smart agriculture and HVAC systems.
- **Motion/Proximity Sensors (e.g., PIR, ultrasonic sensors):** Detect motion for security and automation.
- **Light Sensors (e.g., LDR, TSL2561):** Enable automatic lighting adjustments.
- **Gas Sensors (e.g., MQ-series):** Monitor air quality, detect smoke, or hazardous gases.
- **Pressure Sensors (e.g., BMP280):** Measure atmospheric pressure for weather forecasting and altitude tracking.
- **Accelerometers and Gyroscopes (e.g., MPU6050):** Track movement and orientation in wearable and industrial IoT. These sensors provide the foundational data needed for smart decision-making in IoT systems."

Beginner Tip: Focus on remembering a few key sensors like temperature, humidity, and motion sensors—they appear in almost every IoT project.

Final Thought: Knowing common IoT sensors shows that you understand how IoT devices gather real-world information essential for automation, monitoring, and control.

Interview Question 31: How Does a Temperature Sensor Work?

Why This Question Is Asked: Interviewers want to assess if you understand the basic principles behind one of the most commonly used sensors in IoT and embedded systems.

What the Interviewer Wants to Know:

- Can you explain how a temperature sensor measures temperature?
- Do you know the types of temperature sensors and their methods?
- Can you give practical examples?

How to Structure Your Answer:

1. Briefly explain the principle behind temperature sensors
2. Mention types of temperature sensors (e.g., analog, digital, thermistor, thermocouple)
3. Provide examples and use cases

Sample Answer (Beginner): "A temperature sensor measures heat or cold in the environment and converts it into an electrical signal. Some sensors, like the LM35, create a voltage that changes with temperature. Others, like the DS18B20, give a digital reading directly. These sensors are used in smart thermostats, weather stations, and refrigerators."

Sample Answer (Experienced): "Temperature sensors detect changes in temperature and convert these changes into electrical signals. Analog temperature sensors (e.g., LM35) produce a voltage proportional to the temperature, while digital sensors (e.g., DS18B20) provide a digital output directly via communication protocols like 1-Wire. Other types include thermocouples (which generate a voltage based on temperature difference) and RTDs (which change resistance with temperature). These sensors are widely used in HVAC systems, industrial process monitoring, smart homes, and wearable devices."

Beginner Tip: Think of a temperature sensor as "feeling" the heat or cold and sending a number that represents it.

Final Thought: Understanding how temperature sensors work is essential because temperature monitoring is a core part of many IoT, industrial, and consumer applications.

Interview Question 32: What Is a Humidity Sensor?

Why This Question Is Asked: Interviewers want to check if you understand how devices can measure the amount of moisture in the air, which is critical for many environmental and industrial IoT applications.

What the Interviewer Wants to Know:

- Can you define what a humidity sensor is?
- Do you understand how it works?
- Can you provide real-world examples of its use?

How to Structure Your Answer:
1. Define what a humidity sensor is
2. Explain how it measures humidity
3. Mention examples and applications

Sample Answer (Beginner): "A humidity sensor measures the amount of water vapor in the air. It usually sends an electrical signal based on the moisture it detects. For example, a DHT22 sensor measures both humidity and temperature and is used in weather stations and smart greenhouses."

Sample Answer (Experienced): "A humidity sensor, also called a hygrometer, detects and measures the moisture content (humidity) in the air. It typically works by sensing changes in electrical properties, such as capacitance or resistance, that vary with humidity levels. Capacitive humidity sensors use a moisture-sensitive dielectric material between two electrodes, while resistive sensors measure changes in electrical resistance. Examples include the DHT11, DHT22, and SHT31 sensors, widely used in HVAC systems, smart agriculture, and environmental monitoring."

Beginner Tip: Think of a humidity sensor as a "moisture detector" for the air.

Final Thought: Understanding humidity sensors is important because they play a crucial role in creating comfortable living environments, optimizing industrial processes, and protecting sensitive equipment from moisture damage.

Interview Question 33: How Is Motion Detected in IoT Devices?

Why This Question Is Asked: Interviewers want to assess if you understand the different methods and sensors used to detect motion in IoT applications like security systems, smart lighting, and automation.

What the Interviewer Wants to Know:

- Can you explain how motion detection works?
- Do you know the types of sensors commonly used?
- Can you provide real-world examples?

How to Structure Your Answer:

1. Explain the basic idea of motion detection
2. Mention common types of motion sensors
3. Provide example applications

Sample Answer (Beginner): "Motion in IoT devices is usually detected with special sensors like PIR (Passive Infrared) sensors. PIR sensors sense changes in infrared radiation when a warm body, like a person, moves in front of them. Other sensors like ultrasonic or microwave sensors can also be used. For example, PIR sensors are used in smart lights that turn on when someone enters a room."

Sample Answer (Experienced): "Motion detection in IoT devices is typically achieved using various types of sensors:

- **PIR (Passive Infrared) Sensors**: Detect changes in infrared radiation caused by the movement of warm objects like humans or animals.
- **Ultrasonic Sensors**: Emit sound waves and measure the time it takes for the waves to bounce back from nearby objects.
- **Microwave Sensors**: Use microwave pulses and detect motion based on the Doppler effect.
- **Accelerometers**: Detect motion or vibration in wearable and

portable devices. Each technology is chosen based on the required detection range, power consumption, and environmental conditions. Common use cases include smart security systems, automatic lighting, and smart doorbells."

Beginner Tip: Remember: PIR sensors = detect body heat movement; Ultrasonic = detect objects with sound waves.

Final Thought: Understanding motion detection techniques is important because they are fundamental to automation, security, and energy-saving applications in IoT systems.

Interview Question 34: What Is a PIR Sensor?

Why This Question Is Asked: Interviewers want to see if you understand one of the most commonly used motion detection sensors in IoT and security applications.

What the Interviewer Wants to Know:

- Can you define a PIR sensor?
- Do you know how it works?
- Can you provide example uses?

How to Structure Your Answer:

1. Define what a PIR sensor is
2. Explain how it detects motion
3. Mention real-world applications

Sample Answer (Beginner): "A PIR (Passive Infrared) sensor detects motion by sensing changes in infrared radiation, like body heat. It doesn't emit anything; it only senses. When a person moves past the sensor, it picks up the change in heat and triggers an action, like turning on a light or sounding an alarm."

Sample Answer (Experienced): "A PIR (Passive Infrared) sensor is an electronic sensor that detects infrared (IR) radiation emitted by objects, especially living beings. It measures changes in infrared levels within its field of view to detect motion. PIR sensors are energy-efficient, inexpensive, and commonly used in IoT applications like smart lighting systems, intruder alarms, and occupancy monitoring. They are ideal for detecting human presence without active scanning or high power consumption."

Beginner Tip: Think of a PIR sensor as a "heat movement detector."

Final Thought: Understanding PIR sensors is essential because they are a core component in many smart home, security, and energy-efficient IoT applications.

Interview Question 35: What Is a GPS Module and How Is It Used in IoT?

Why This Question Is Asked: Interviewers want to check if you understand how location tracking works in IoT devices and why GPS is critical in many real-world applications.

What the Interviewer Wants to Know:

- Can you define a GPS module?
- Do you understand how it works?
- Can you explain how GPS modules are applied in IoT?

How to Structure Your Answer:

1. Define what a GPS module is
2. Explain how it determines location
3. Mention IoT applications where GPS is used

Sample Answer (Beginner): "A GPS module is a device that connects to satellites to find out where it is on Earth. It tells the exact location (latitude, longitude) of the device. In IoT, GPS modules are used in things like vehicle trackers, pet trackers, and delivery drones."

Sample Answer (Experienced): "A GPS (Global Positioning System) module receives signals from a network of satellites to calculate its precise geographic location (latitude, longitude, and altitude). In IoT applications, GPS modules are integrated into systems requiring real-time location tracking, such as fleet management, asset tracking, smart agriculture (for equipment tracking), personal fitness devices, and geofencing-based automation. GPS modules like the NEO-6M or SIM808 are commonly used for low-power, reliable positioning solutions in mobile and remote IoT deployments."

Beginner Tip: Think of a GPS module as a "location finder" for IoT devices.

Final Thought: Understanding GPS modules is crucial because many IoT applications depend on accurate, real-time location data to provide smart tracking, navigation, and automation solutions.

Interview Question 36: How Do You Interface a Sensor with a Microcontroller?

Why This Question Is Asked: Interviewers want to assess if you understand the practical steps involved in connecting sensors to microcontrollers, a fundamental skill for IoT and embedded system projects.

What the Interviewer Wants to Know:

- Can you describe the basic process of interfacing a sensor?
- Do you know the hardware and software steps?
- Can you explain using simple examples?

How to Structure Your Answer:

1. Explain the general hardware steps
2. Describe basic software/programming steps
3. Mention an example of a simple sensor connection

Sample Answer (Beginner): "To connect a sensor to a microcontroller, you first connect the sensor's power (VCC) and ground (GND) pins to the microcontroller's power and ground. Then you connect the sensor's output pin to one of the microcontroller's input pins. In code, you read the sensor's data through that input pin. For example, to connect a temperature sensor like LM35 to an Arduino, you use an analog pin to read its voltage and convert it to temperature."

Sample Answer (Experienced): "Interfacing a sensor with a microcontroller involves:

1. **Hardware Connections**: Connect sensor VCC to microcontroller VCC, GND to GND, and the sensor output to a suitable GPIO, ADC, or communication interface (I2C, SPI, UART).
2. **Initialization**: Configure the microcontroller's pin modes and communication protocols if needed.
3. **Data Acquisition**: Read data either by polling (for simple sensors) or interrupt-driven methods (for real-time systems).
4. **Processing**: Apply calibration or scaling to the raw sensor data. For example, using an I2C temperature sensor like BMP280 with an STM32 involves configuring the I2C bus, sending a read command, and interpreting the digital data returned by the sensor."

Beginner Tip: Start with sensors that offer simple analog or digital outputs before moving to advanced protocols like I2C and SPI.

Final Thought: Knowing how to interface sensors with microcontrollers shows that you can bridge the physical and digital worlds—a vital skill in building functional IoT and embedded systems.

Interview Question 37: What Is an ADC and How Is It Used?

Why This Question Is Asked: Interviewers want to verify if you understand how analog signals are converted into digital data that microcontrollers and computers can process.

What the Interviewer Wants to Know:

- Can you define an ADC?
- Do you understand why ADCs are needed?
- Can you explain where and how ADCs are used?

How to Structure Your Answer:

1. Define ADC simply
2. Explain its purpose
3. Provide examples of where it is used

Sample Answer (Beginner): "ADC stands for Analog-to-Digital Converter. It changes a signal like voltage from a sensor into a number that a microcontroller can understand. For example, when a temperature sensor gives an analog voltage, an ADC converts that into a digital value that shows the temperature."

Sample Answer (Experienced): "An ADC (Analog-to-Digital Converter) is an electronic component that converts continuous analog signals into discrete digital numbers for processing by digital systems like microcontrollers. It samples the input signal at regular intervals and quantizes the amplitude into a finite set of digital levels. ADCs are essential in IoT applications for reading data from analog sensors such as temperature sensors (LM35), light sensors (LDRs), and pressure sensors (MPX5700). Most microcontrollers like STM32, Arduino, and ESP32 come with built-in ADC modules to facilitate easy sensor interfacing."

Beginner Tip: Think of an ADC as a "translator" that helps a microcontroller "understand" real-world signals.

Final Thought: Understanding ADCs is fundamental because most real-world signals are analog, and IoT systems need digital data for processing, decision-making, and control.

Interview Question 38: What Is a DAC and Its Application in IoT?

Why This Question Is Asked: Interviewers want to know if you understand how digital systems can output analog signals, which is essential for controlling real-world devices in IoT applications.

What the Interviewer Wants to Know:

- Can you define a DAC?
- Do you understand why and when it is used?
- Can you give examples of DAC applications in IoT?

How to Structure Your Answer:

1. Define DAC simply
2. Explain its purpose
3. Provide examples of use in IoT

Sample Answer (Beginner): "DAC stands for Digital-to-Analog Converter. It changes digital numbers from a microcontroller into real-world analog signals, like voltages. In IoT, DACs are used to control things like the brightness of lights, the speed of motors, or the volume of speakers."

Sample Answer (Experienced): "A DAC (Digital-to-Analog Converter) converts digital data (typically binary) from a microcontroller into a corresponding continuous analog voltage or current. DACs are crucial in IoT applications requiring analog control or outputs, such as generating audio signals in smart speakers, controlling actuator positions (e.g., servo motors), regulating analog sensors in industrial automation, and simulating sensor outputs for testing. Common DAC implementations are found in microcontrollers like STM32, ESP32, or external DAC chips like MCP4725."

Beginner Tip: Think of a DAC as the "reverse" of an ADC: it takes digital info and turns it into a real-world signal.

Final Thought: Understanding DACs is important because many IoT applications need to interact with analog components, not just read them—and DACs make that possible.

Interview Question 39: How Are Actuators Controlled in IoT?

Why This Question Is Asked: Interviewers want to assess if you understand the basic mechanisms behind controlling real-world actions through IoT systems.

What the Interviewer Wants to Know:

- Can you explain how actuators receive and respond to commands?
- Do you know the methods of controlling actuators (digital vs analog signals)?
- Can you give examples of IoT actuator control applications?

How to Structure Your Answer:

1. Define actuator control in simple terms
2. Mention control methods (digital signals, PWM, analog signals)
3. Provide real-world examples

Sample Answer (Beginner): "Actuators in IoT are controlled by sending signals from a microcontroller. For example, to turn on a motor, the controller sends an electrical signal through a pin. Some actuators are controlled with simple ON/OFF signals, while others need more complex signals like PWM to control speed or position. Examples include smart door locks or robotic arms."

Sample Answer (Experienced): "Actuators in IoT systems are controlled using:

- **Digital Signals**: ON/OFF control (e.g., turning a relay on or off).
- **Analog Signals**: Using DACs to output variable voltages to analog

actuators.

- **PWM (Pulse Width Modulation)**: For controlling motors, servos, or LED brightness by varying duty cycles. Commands are typically triggered by sensor data, cloud-based instructions, or pre-programmed events. Examples include controlling HVAC dampers in smart buildings, adjusting irrigation valves in smart farming, and operating servos in smart robots."

Beginner Tip: Remember: sensors collect information, and actuators "act" based on decisions made by the controller.

Final Thought: Understanding how actuators are controlled is crucial for designing complete IoT systems that can sense the environment and physically respond to it.

Interview Question 40: What Is a Relay and How Is It Used?

Why This Question Is Asked: Interviewers want to ensure you understand basic switching mechanisms that allow low-power IoT devices to control high-power equipment safely.

What the Interviewer Wants to Know:

- Can you define a relay?
- Do you understand how it works?
- Can you explain real-world uses in IoT?

How to Structure Your Answer:

1. Define a relay simply
2. Explain how it operates (electromagnetic switching)
3. Provide examples of relay use in IoT

Sample Answer (Beginner): "A relay is an electrically operated switch. It uses a small electrical signal from a microcontroller to turn on or off a larger current, like controlling a light or fan. In IoT, relays are used to control home appliances remotely, like turning on a water pump from a smartphone app."

Sample Answer (Experienced): "A relay is an electromechanical or solid-state device that uses a low-power control signal to operate a high-power electrical circuit. Electromagnetic relays use a coil to create a magnetic field that moves a switch, while solid-state relays use semiconductor switching. In IoT systems, relays allow microcontrollers like Arduino or ESP32 to safely control high-voltage devices such as HVAC systems, home lighting, industrial machinery, and irrigation systems. They are critical for isolating low-voltage control circuits from dangerous high-voltage circuits."

Beginner Tip: Think of a relay as a "remote control switch" that lets a small controller operate big electrical loads.

Final Thought: Understanding relays is essential because they allow IoT devices to bridge the gap between low-power electronics and real-world high-power systems safely and effectively.

Interview Question 41: What Is I2C Communication?

Why This Question Is Asked: Interviewers want to assess if you understand one of the most common communication protocols used to connect multiple sensors and devices in IoT systems.

What the Interviewer Wants to Know:
- Can you define I2C?
- Do you understand how it works (master-slave communication)?
- Can you mention where it is typically used?

How to Structure Your Answer:
1. Define I2C simply
2. Explain how it works (two-wire interface: SDA, SCL)
3. Provide examples of I2C applications

Sample Answer (Beginner): "I2C, which stands for Inter-Integrated Circuit, is a communication method that lets a microcontroller talk to multiple sensors or devices using just two wires: one for data (SDA) and one for clock (SCL). It is often used to connect things like temperature sensors, displays, and accelerometers to a microcontroller."

Sample Answer (Experienced): "I2C (Inter-Integrated Circuit) is a synchronous, multi-master, multi-slave serial communication protocol that uses only two bidirectional lines: SDA (Serial Data Line) and SCL (Serial Clock Line). It enables efficient communication between a master device (usually a microcontroller) and multiple slave devices (sensors, memory chips, displays) by addressing each slave uniquely. I2C is widely used in IoT for connecting low-speed peripherals like OLED displays (SSD1306), environmental sensors (BMP280), and real-time clocks (DS3231). Its simplicity and scalability make it ideal for embedded systems."

Beginner Tip: Remember: two wires (SDA and SCL) can connect many devices without using lots of pins.

Final Thought: Understanding I2C communication is crucial because it allows you to efficiently expand your IoT projects without needing extra wiring or complex interfaces.

Interview Question 42: What Is SPI Communication?

Why This Question Is Asked: Interviewers want to verify if you understand another important communication protocol used in IoT and embedded systems for high-speed device communication.

What the Interviewer Wants to Know:

- Can you define SPI?
- Do you understand how it works (master-slave, multi-wire connection)?
- Can you mention typical uses?

How to Structure Your Answer:

1. Define SPI simply
2. Explain how it works (four main signals)
3. Provide examples of SPI applications

Sample Answer (Beginner): "SPI stands for Serial Peripheral Interface. It is a communication method that uses four wires: one for sending data, one for receiving data, one for clock signals, and one to select the device. It is often used to connect things like memory cards, displays, and sensors to microcontrollers."

Sample Answer (Experienced): "SPI (Serial Peripheral Interface) is a synchronous serial communication protocol primarily used for high-speed, short-distance communication between a master device (typically a microcontroller) and one or more slave devices. It uses four lines: MOSI (Master Out Slave In), MISO (Master In Slave Out), SCLK (Serial Clock), and SS/CS (Slave Select/Chip Select). SPI is commonly used in IoT systems for connecting high-speed peripherals such as flash memory (e.g., EEPROMs), LCD displays, SD cards, and high-resolution sensors. It provides faster data rates than I2C but typically requires more wiring."

Beginner Tip: Remember: SPI = faster but needs more wires than I2C.

Final Thought: Understanding SPI communication is key because it enables fast and efficient data transfer between microcontrollers and high-performance peripherals in IoT systems.

Interview Question 43: What Is UART and Where Is It Used?

Why This Question Is Asked: Interviewers want to check if you understand a very basic and widely-used method of serial communication essential for many IoT and embedded projects.

What the Interviewer Wants to Know:

- Can you define UART?
- Do you know how it works (serial, asynchronous communication)?
- Can you provide examples where UART is used?

How to Structure Your Answer:

1. Define UART simply
2. Explain how it works (asynchronous, two-wire communication)
3. Provide examples of its applications

Sample Answer (Beginner): "UART stands for Universal Asynchronous Receiver/Transmitter. It is a way for two devices to send and receive data one bit at a time over two wires—one for sending (TX) and one for receiving (RX). It's often used to connect microcontrollers with modules like Bluetooth modules (HC-05) or GPS receivers."

Sample Answer (Experienced): "UART (Universal Asynchronous Receiver/Transmitter) is a hardware communication protocol that enables asynchronous, serial communication between devices without the need for a clock signal. Data is transmitted bit-by-bit through two lines: TX (Transmit) and RX (Receive), along with a predefined baud rate for timing synchronization. UART is widely used in IoT for interfacing modules such as GPS receivers (e.g., NEO-6M), GSM/GPRS modules (e.g., SIM800L), Bluetooth modules (e.g., HC-05/HC-06), and for debugging purposes via serial consoles."

Beginner Tip: Remember: UART is "simple, two-wire, and asynchronous," and it's great for many common IoT modules.

Final Thought: Understanding UART is important because it forms the backbone of basic serial communication between microcontrollers and peripheral devices in countless IoT systems.

Interview Question 44: How Do You Power IoT Devices Efficiently?

Why This Question Is Asked: Interviewers want to assess if you understand the critical role of energy management in IoT design, especially for battery-powered and remote devices.

What the Interviewer Wants to Know:

- Can you explain strategies for minimizing power consumption?
- Do you know different power sources and techniques used in IoT?
- Can you give examples of best practices?

How to Structure Your Answer:

1. Explain why efficient powering is important
2. Mention key strategies and technologies
3. Provide practical examples

Sample Answer (Beginner): "To power IoT devices efficiently, you use low-power components and put devices into sleep mode when they are not doing anything. You can also use batteries, solar panels, or energy harvesting. For example, a weather station can run for years on a small battery if it only wakes up once every hour to send data."

Sample Answer (Experienced): "Efficient powering of IoT devices involves using low-power microcontrollers (e.g., ARM Cortex-M0+), optimizing software to enable deep sleep or low-power modes, duty cycling (waking up only to perform tasks), and choosing appropriate power sources such as batteries, solar panels, or energy harvesting systems. Additionally, communication protocols like LoRaWAN and BLE are selected for their low energy demands. Techniques like local edge processing also reduce the need for continuous cloud communication, conserving energy. Examples include remote environmental sensors powered by small solar cells combined with supercapacitors or long-life lithium batteries."

Beginner Tip: Always look for "low-power" components and use "sleep modes" whenever possible.

Final Thought: Efficient power management is key for creating scalable, long-lasting, and reliable IoT systems, especially when devices are deployed in hard-to-reach areas.

Interview Question 45: What Are Low-Power Microcontrollers?

Why This Question Is Asked: Interviewers want to assess if you understand the importance of choosing the right microcontrollers for energy-efficient IoT systems.

What the Interviewer Wants to Know:

- Can you define low-power microcontrollers?
- Do you understand why they are important in IoT?
- Can you give examples?

How to Structure Your Answer:

1. Define low-power microcontrollers simply
2. Explain their features and importance
3. Provide examples and use cases

Sample Answer (Beginner): "Low-power microcontrollers are special chips that use very little energy, especially when they are sleeping or not working. They are important in IoT because many devices need to run for a long time on small batteries. Examples include the Arduino Pro Mini and STM32L series."

Sample Answer (Experienced): "Low-power microcontrollers are specially designed MCUs optimized to operate at extremely low current levels, particularly in standby or sleep modes, to extend battery life in IoT and embedded applications. They often support features like multiple sleep modes, low-voltage operation, quick wake-up times, and optimized peripheral management. Examples include the STM32L0/L4 series, Nordic Semiconductor's nRF52 series (for BLE), and Atmel's SAM L21 series. These microcontrollers are widely used in wearables, remote sensors, healthcare devices, and smart agriculture solutions."

Beginner Tip: If your IoT device needs to run on batteries for a long time, always consider using a low-power MCU.

Final Thought: Understanding low-power microcontrollers is crucial for building energy-efficient, reliable IoT solutions that can operate for months or even years without maintenance.

Interview Question 46: What Is Energy Harvesting in IoT?

Why This Question Is Asked: Interviewers want to know if you understand modern techniques that allow IoT devices to operate independently by generating their own power from the environment.

What the Interviewer Wants to Know:

- Can you define energy harvesting?
- Do you know why it's important in IoT?
- Can you give examples of energy sources and applications?

How to Structure Your Answer:

1. Define energy harvesting simply
2. Explain its importance for IoT
3. Provide examples of energy sources and practical uses

Sample Answer (Beginner): "Energy harvesting means collecting small amounts of energy from the environment, like sunlight or motion, and using it to power IoT devices. This way, the devices don't need big batteries or wires. For example, solar-powered sensors in a smart farm can work for years without needing battery changes."

Sample Answer (Experienced): "Energy harvesting in IoT refers to capturing ambient energy from natural or artificial sources—such as solar, thermal gradients, vibration, or radio frequency (RF) signals—and converting it into electrical power to run low-power devices. This approach reduces the need for frequent battery replacements and enables maintenance-free operation in remote or inaccessible locations.

Applications include solar-powered environmental sensors, piezoelectric energy harvesting in wearable devices, and RF harvesting for wireless sensor networks. Energy harvesting is crucial for sustainable and scalable IoT deployments."

Beginner Tip: Think of energy harvesting as "charging a device using free energy from the surroundings."

Final Thought: Understanding energy harvesting is vital for designing next-generation IoT systems that are self-powered, eco-friendly, and capable of long-term, unattended operation.

Interview Question 47: How Does Wireless Charging Work for IoT?

Why This Question Is Asked: Interviewers want to assess if you understand advanced power delivery methods for IoT devices, especially for applications where physical connectors are impractical.

What the Interviewer Wants to Know:

- Can you explain the principle behind wireless charging?
- Do you understand its advantages and limitations?
- Can you give examples of where it is applied in IoT?

How to Structure Your Answer:

1. Explain the basic principle (electromagnetic induction)
2. Describe how it is used for charging IoT devices
3. Provide examples and practical applications

Sample Answer (Beginner): "Wireless charging uses magnetic fields to transfer energy between a charger and a device without using wires. In IoT, it is helpful for devices like smartwatches, wireless sensors, or medical implants where plugging in is difficult."

Sample Answer (Experienced): "Wireless charging for IoT typically uses electromagnetic induction or resonant inductive coupling to transfer power wirelessly between a transmitter coil (in the charging base) and a receiver coil (in the device). It enables sealed, waterproof, and maintenance-free designs ideal for harsh environments. Applications include charging wearable devices, implanted medical sensors, industrial IoT devices in hazardous areas, and wireless charging docks for mobile robots. Challenges include energy transfer efficiency, alignment precision, and short operational distances."

Beginner Tip: Think of wireless charging as "moving energy through the air" using magnetic fields instead of cables.

Final Thought: Understanding wireless charging is important because it enables new designs for IoT devices that are safer, more reliable, and easier to maintain, especially in challenging environments.

Interview Question 48: What Are Wearables in the Context of IoT?

Why This Question Is Asked: Interviewers want to assess if you understand how personal devices are integrated into the IoT ecosystem to collect, process, and share real-time data.

What the Interviewer Wants to Know:

- Can you define what wearables are?
- Do you understand their role in IoT?
- Can you provide examples?

How to Structure Your Answer:

1. Define wearables simply
2. Explain their connection to IoT
3. Mention common examples and applications

Sample Answer (Beginner): "Wearables are smart electronic devices that people wear, like smartwatches and fitness trackers. They collect data like heart rate, steps, or sleep patterns and often send it to a smartphone or cloud for analysis. They are part of IoT because they connect to the internet and share data."

Sample Answer (Experienced): "Wearables in IoT refer to smart, body-worn electronic devices embedded with sensors, software, and connectivity features that continuously monitor, collect, and transmit data about the user or their surroundings. They typically use wireless communication protocols like Bluetooth or Wi-Fi to sync with smartphones or cloud platforms. Examples include fitness trackers (e.g., Fitbit), smartwatches (e.g., Apple Watch), wearable ECG monitors, smart glasses, and health monitoring patches. Wearables play a critical role in healthcare, sports analytics, personal safety, and augmented reality applications."

Beginner Tip: Think of wearables as "smart gadgets you wear that talk to other devices through the internet."

Final Thought: Understanding wearables is important because they represent one of the fastest-growing and most impactful sectors in the IoT ecosystem, directly connecting technology to daily human activity.

Interview Question 49: What Are the Advantages of Using ESP32 or ESP8266?

Why This Question Is Asked: Interviewers want to assess if you are familiar with popular microcontrollers in IoT development and can explain why they are widely chosen for projects.

What the Interviewer Wants to Know:

- Can you highlight the key features of ESP32 and ESP8266?
- Do you understand their advantages in IoT applications?
- Can you provide use-case examples?

How to Structure Your Answer:

1. Introduce ESP32 and ESP8266 briefly
2. Mention their advantages
3. Give practical examples where they are commonly used

Sample Answer (Beginner): "The ESP32 and ESP8266 are small microcontrollers with built-in Wi-Fi. The ESP32 also has Bluetooth. They are cheap, powerful, and perfect for IoT projects like home automation and weather stations. They are easy to program using Arduino IDE."

Sample Answer (Experienced): "The ESP8266 and ESP32 are low-cost, highly integrated Wi-Fi microcontrollers widely used in IoT development. Advantages include:

- **Built-in Wi-Fi (and Bluetooth for ESP32):** Simplifies connectivity without external modules.
- **Low Power Consumption:** Features like deep sleep modes support energy-efficient designs.
- **High Processing Power:** Especially ESP32 with dual-core processors and real-time capabilities.
- **Rich Peripheral Support:** GPIOs, ADCs, DACs, PWM, UART, SPI, I2C, and more.
- **Large Community and Open-Source Support:** Extensive libraries, examples, and community forums. Typical applications include smart home automation, wireless sensor networks, remote monitoring systems, and wearable devices."

Beginner Tip: If you want to build IoT projects with Wi-Fi easily and cheaply, ESP8266 and ESP32 are great starting points.

Final Thought: Knowing the advantages of ESP32 and ESP8266 shows that you are familiar with practical, accessible hardware choices for powerful and connected IoT solutions.

Interview Question 50: What Is GPIO and How Is It Used?

Why This Question Is Asked: Interviewers want to see if you understand how microcontrollers interact with external components through simple input and output operations.

What the Interviewer Wants to Know:
- Can you define GPIO?
- Do you know how GPIOs are used in IoT and embedded systems?
- Can you give real-world examples?

How to Structure Your Answer:
1. Define GPIO simply
2. Explain its basic functions (input/output)
3. Provide practical examples

Sample Answer (Beginner): "GPIO stands for General Purpose Input/Output. These are pins on a microcontroller that you can program to either read information from a sensor (input) or control something like an LED (output). For example, you can connect a button to a GPIO pin and read if it's pressed."

Sample Answer (Experienced): "GPIO (General Purpose Input/Output) refers to configurable pins on a microcontroller that can act either as digital inputs (to read states like button presses or sensor signals) or digital outputs (to control devices like LEDs, relays, or buzzers). GPIOs are essential for interfacing with external peripherals, implementing control logic, and responding to physical events. For instance, a GPIO pin configured as input can detect motion via a PIR sensor, while an output GPIO can trigger a relay to turn on a light in a smart home system."

Beginner Tip: Think of GPIOs as the "hands and ears" of a microcontroller—they help it interact with the outside world.

Final Thought: Understanding GPIO usage is fundamental because it forms the basis of connecting and controlling physical devices in any embedded or IoT project.

Section 3: Networking & Protocols (51–75)

Interview Question 51: What Is an IP Address?

Why This Question Is Asked: Interviewers want to check if you understand the basic concept of networking, which is essential for connecting IoT devices across the internet.

What the Interviewer Wants to Know:

- Can you define an IP address?
- Do you understand its role in device communication?
- Can you mention types of IP addresses?

How to Structure Your Answer:

1. Define IP address simply
2. Explain why it is important
3. Mention types (IPv4, IPv6, static, dynamic)

Sample Answer (Beginner): "An IP address is like a home address for a device on a network. It tells other devices where to send data. Without an IP address, devices couldn't find or talk to each other."

Sample Answer (Experienced): "An IP (Internet Protocol) address is a unique numerical identifier assigned to each device connected to a network. It enables devices to locate, communicate, and exchange data with each other across the internet or local networks. There are two main versions: IPv4 (e.g., 192.168.1.1) and IPv6 (e.g., 2001:db8::1), with IPv6 developed to accommodate the growing number of devices. IP addresses can also be static (fixed) or dynamic (assigned temporarily by a DHCP server). In IoT, IP addresses allow sensors, actuators, and gateways to interact across cloud platforms and remote systems."

Beginner Tip: Think of an IP address as the "name tag" that lets devices find and talk to each other.

Final Thought: Understanding IP addresses is crucial because every connected IoT device needs one to communicate with cloud services, mobile apps, and other smart devices.

Interview Question 52: What Is IPv6 and Why Is It Important for IoT?

Why This Question Is Asked: Interviewers want to assess if you understand why modern IoT systems depend on IPv6 for future scalability and connectivity.

What the Interviewer Wants to Know:
- Can you define IPv6?
- Do you know why IPv6 is critical for IoT growth?
- Can you mention benefits compared to IPv4?

How to Structure Your Answer:
1. Define IPv6 simply
2. Explain why it matters for IoT
3. Highlight key advantages

Sample Answer (Beginner): "IPv6 is the newest version of the internet address system. It gives a lot more addresses than the old IPv4 system. In IoT, we need many addresses because there are so many smart devices, and IPv6 makes sure every device can have its own address."

Sample Answer (Experienced): "IPv6 (Internet Protocol version 6) is the next-generation IP addressing protocol designed to replace IPv4. It provides a vastly larger address space (2^{128} addresses) compared to IPv4, which is crucial for accommodating the explosive growth of IoT devices. IPv6 also offers improved routing efficiency, built-in security features (IPsec), and better support for mobile and low-power devices. In IoT ecosystems, IPv6 ensures that every sensor, actuator, and gateway can have a unique address, enabling seamless end-to-end communication without relying on NAT (Network Address Translation)."

Beginner Tip: Think of IPv6 as "giving every IoT device its own unique house address on the internet."

Final Thought: Understanding IPv6 is critical because IoT networks must scale to billions of devices, and only IPv6 can provide the addressing and flexibility needed for that growth.

Interview Question 53: What Is DNS?

Why This Question Is Asked: Interviewers want to assess if you understand how devices find each other over the internet—a basic but critical networking concept for IoT communication.

What the Interviewer Wants to Know:
- Can you define DNS?
- Do you understand how it helps in networking?
- Can you explain its relevance to IoT?

How to Structure Your Answer:
1. Define DNS simply
2. Explain its purpose (name-to-IP translation)
3. Provide examples and IoT relevance

Sample Answer (Beginner): "DNS stands for Domain Name System. It works like a phonebook for the internet. When you type a website name like www.google.com, DNS finds the right IP address so your computer or IoT device knows where to connect."

Sample Answer (Experienced): "The Domain Name System (DNS) is a distributed database that translates human-readable domain names (e.g., www.example.com) into machine-readable IP addresses (e.g., 192.0.2.1). It simplifies communication by allowing users and devices to use friendly names instead of remembering numerical IP addresses. In IoT, DNS is critical for connecting devices to cloud services, APIs, and remote servers without hard-coding IP addresses, enabling flexible and scalable deployments. DNS also supports service discovery mechanisms in dynamic IoT environments."

Beginner Tip: Think of DNS as the "directory service" that finds the right location for devices or websites.

Final Thought: Understanding DNS is important because every time an IoT device sends data to the cloud or accesses a service, it often relies on DNS to find its destination.

Interview Question 54: What Are the Layers of the OSI Model?

Why This Question Is Asked: Interviewers want to check if you understand the standardized model that explains how data moves across a network—essential for troubleshooting and designing IoT communication systems.

What the Interviewer Wants to Know:

- Can you list and explain the seven OSI layers?
- Do you understand each layer's role?
- Can you link them to real-world examples?

How to Structure Your Answer:

1. List the seven layers in order
2. Briefly explain the function of each
3. Provide simple real-world examples

Sample Answer (Beginner): "The OSI model has seven layers:

1. **Physical**: Moves raw bits (example: cables, Wi-Fi signals)
2. **Data Link**: Moves frames between devices (example: Ethernet)
3. **Network**: Moves packets across networks (example: IP addresses)
4. **Transport**: Makes sure data is delivered properly (example: TCP, UDP)
5. **Session**: Manages connections (example: logins)
6. **Presentation**: Formats and encrypts data (example: JPEG, SSL)
7. **Application**: Interacts with software (example: web browsers, MQTT apps)"

Sample Answer (Experienced): "The OSI (Open Systems Interconnection) model describes network communication in seven layers:

1. **Physical Layer**: Transmits raw binary data (bits) over physical media (e.g., cabling, radio waves).
2. **Data Link Layer**: Handles node-to-node communication and error detection (e.g., MAC addresses, Ethernet).
3. **Network Layer**: Manages logical addressing and routing (e.g., IP protocol).
4. **Transport Layer**: Ensures reliable data delivery and flow control (e.g., TCP, UDP).
5. **Session Layer**: Establishes, maintains, and terminates sessions between devices (e.g., RPC).
6. **Presentation Layer**: Translates, encrypts, and compresses data (e.g., SSL/TLS, JPEG).
7. **Application Layer**: Provides services directly to user applications (e.g., HTTP, FTP, MQTT). The OSI model helps IoT developers and network engineers diagnose and build efficient communication systems."

Beginner Tip: Use the memory trick: **"Please Do Not Throw Sausage Pizza Away"** (Physical, Data Link, Network, Transport, Session, Presentation, Application).

Final Thought: Understanding the OSI model is crucial because it gives you a clear structure for how devices communicate, making it easier to troubleshoot and design IoT networks.

Interview Question 55: How Does the TCP/IP Model Differ from the OSI Model?

Why This Question Is Asked: Interviewers want to test if you can differentiate between the two foundational networking models and understand real-world communication architecture.

What the Interviewer Wants to Know:

- Can you explain both models?
- Do you understand key differences?
- Can you relate it to IoT or real networking scenarios?

How to Structure Your Answer:

1. Briefly describe both models
2. Highlight major differences
3. Provide examples and practical relevance

Sample Answer (Beginner): "The OSI model has seven layers and is a theoretical guide. The TCP/IP model has four layers and is used in real-world internet communication. TCP/IP is simpler and combines some OSI layers together, like combining Application, Presentation, and Session into one Application layer."

Sample Answer (Experienced): "The OSI model is a conceptual framework with seven layers (Physical, Data Link, Network, Transport, Session, Presentation, Application) designed to standardize networking communication. The TCP/IP model, on the other hand, is a practical implementation with four layers: Link, Internet, Transport, and Application. Key differences include:

- **Number of Layers**: OSI has 7, TCP/IP has 4.
- **Usage**: OSI is mainly theoretical; TCP/IP drives real-world internet communication.
- **Layer Mapping**: OSI's Application, Presentation, and Session layers are combined into TCP/IP's Application layer. In IoT, most devices and networks are built following the TCP/IP stack for interoperability with the internet and cloud platforms."

Beginner Tip: Remember: OSI = "ideal model," TCP/IP = "real-world system."

Final Thought: Knowing how TCP/IP differs from OSI helps you understand the theoretical basis of networking and how it translates into real, practical IoT systems.

Interview Question 56: What Is HTTP vs HTTPS?

Why This Question Is Asked: Interviewers want to assess if you understand basic web communication protocols, especially in terms of security—a key concern for IoT systems that interact with the internet.

What the Interviewer Wants to Know:

- Can you define HTTP and HTTPS?
- Do you know the key difference (security)?
- Can you explain why HTTPS is preferred?

How to Structure Your Answer:

1. Define HTTP and HTTPS simply
2. Explain the main difference (encryption)
3. Mention practical uses and importance for IoT

Sample Answer (Beginner): "HTTP stands for Hypertext Transfer Protocol and is used to send data over the web. HTTPS is the same but with extra security—it uses encryption to protect the data. HTTPS is important for IoT because it keeps information safe from hackers."

Sample Answer (Experienced): "HTTP (Hypertext Transfer Protocol) is an application-layer protocol for transmitting hypermedia (like web pages) over the internet without encryption. HTTPS (Hypertext Transfer Protocol Secure) is the secure version of HTTP that encrypts data using SSL/TLS protocols, protecting data integrity and privacy. In IoT applications, HTTPS is preferred when transmitting sensitive data (e.g., user credentials, sensor readings) to prevent eavesdropping, tampering, and man-in-the-middle attacks."

Beginner Tip: Remember: "HTTPS = HTTP + Security."

Final Thought: Understanding HTTP vs HTTPS is important because secure communication is critical when IoT devices send sensitive data to cloud servers or mobile apps.

Interview Question 57: What Is a RESTful API?

Why This Question Is Asked: Interviewers want to assess if you understand how modern web-based communication works, especially for connecting IoT devices to cloud services.

What the Interviewer Wants to Know:

- Can you define what a RESTful API is?
- Do you understand its principles (HTTP methods, statelessness)?
- Can you explain its use in IoT?

How to Structure Your Answer:
1. Define RESTful API simply
2. Explain its core principles
3. Provide examples and relevance to IoT

Sample Answer (Beginner): "A RESTful API is a way for devices and apps to talk to each other over the internet using simple rules. It uses methods like GET (to get data) and POST (to send data). IoT devices often use RESTful APIs to send sensor data to the cloud."

Sample Answer (Experienced): "A RESTful API (Representational State Transfer API) is a web service that follows REST principles to enable communication between clients and servers over HTTP. It uses standard HTTP methods like GET (retrieve data), POST (create data), PUT (update data), and DELETE (remove data), and is stateless, meaning each request is independent. In IoT, RESTful APIs allow devices to send sensor data to cloud platforms, control actuators remotely, and integrate with third-party services. Examples include IoT platforms like AWS IoT, Azure IoT Hub, and Blynk Cloud."

Beginner Tip: Think of a RESTful API as "rules for devices and servers to understand each other easily over the internet."

Final Thought: Understanding RESTful APIs is crucial because they are the standard way IoT devices communicate with cloud servers, mobile apps, and external services in modern applications.

Interview Question 58: What Is JSON and How Is It Used in IoT?

Why This Question Is Asked: Interviewers want to see if you understand how lightweight data formats like JSON are used for communication in modern IoT applications.

What the Interviewer Wants to Know:
- Can you define JSON?
- Do you know why JSON is important?
- Can you explain how IoT devices use JSON?

How to Structure Your Answer:

1. Define JSON simply
2. Explain why it's useful (lightweight, human-readable)
3. Mention examples in IoT communication

Sample Answer (Beginner): "JSON stands for JavaScript Object Notation. It's a simple way to format and exchange data using key-value pairs. In IoT, devices use JSON to send sensor readings like temperature or humidity to the cloud because it's easy for both machines and people to understand."

Sample Answer (Experienced): "JSON (JavaScript Object Notation) is a lightweight, text-based data format used for structured data exchange between systems. It represents data in key-value pairs and arrays, making it easy to parse and generate. In IoT, JSON is commonly used for sending sensor data, device status updates, and control commands over HTTP or MQTT protocols to cloud servers or mobile apps. Its human-readable nature and minimal overhead make it ideal for resource-constrained IoT devices."

Beginner Tip: Think of JSON as a "simple language" that devices use to talk to cloud platforms and apps.

Final Thought: Understanding JSON is crucial because it is the most common format for IoT data exchange, especially when communicating with APIs and cloud-based services.

Interview Question 59: What Is the Role of Sockets in IoT Communication?

Why This Question Is Asked: Interviewers want to assess if you understand how low-level communication happens between devices over a network in IoT systems.

What the Interviewer Wants to Know:
- Can you define what a socket is?
- Do you know how sockets enable communication?
- Can you give examples of their usage in IoT?

How to Structure Your Answer:
1. Define sockets simply
2. Explain how they work (IP address + port communication)
3. Mention examples of sockets in IoT communication

Sample Answer (Beginner): "A socket is like a door that lets two devices on a network talk to each other. It uses an IP address and a port number to make the connection. In IoT, sockets are used to send data directly between devices, like a weather station sending readings to a server."

Sample Answer (Experienced): "A socket is an endpoint for sending and receiving data across a network, combining an IP address and a port number to create a communication link. In IoT, sockets enable real-time, direct communication between devices, gateways, and cloud servers over TCP or UDP protocols. They are commonly used in applications like remote device monitoring, telemetry, and control systems where efficient, reliable data exchange is critical. Examples include using TCP sockets for secure sensor data transmission or UDP sockets for low-latency, real-time updates in smart home devices."

Beginner Tip: Think of a socket as a "telephone line" that two devices use to talk to each other over the internet.

Final Thought: Understanding sockets is important because they are the foundation of real-time communication in many IoT and networking applications.

Interview Question 60: What Is WebSocket?

Why This Question Is Asked: Interviewers want to assess if you know modern communication technologies that enable real-time, low-latency communication—very important for responsive IoT applications.

What the Interviewer Wants to Know:

- Can you define WebSocket?
- Do you understand how it differs from traditional HTTP?
- Can you explain where it is used in IoT?

How to Structure Your Answer:
1. Define WebSocket simply
2. Explain its main advantage (full-duplex communication)
3. Provide examples of IoT applications using WebSocket

Sample Answer (Beginner): "WebSocket is a way for two devices to keep talking to each other without starting a new connection each time. Once connected, they can send messages back and forth instantly. In IoT, WebSocket is used for things like real-time updates in smart home dashboards."

Sample Answer (Experienced): "WebSocket is a communication protocol that provides full-duplex, persistent connections over a single TCP connection. Unlike traditional HTTP, which follows a request-response model, WebSocket allows both the client and server to send data anytime without re-establishing connections. In IoT, WebSocket is widely used for real-time applications like live sensor dashboards, remote device control panels, and instant alerting systems in smart homes, industrial monitoring, and wearable devices."

Beginner Tip: Think of WebSocket as a "permanent open conversation" between your IoT device and the server.

Final Thought: Understanding WebSocket is crucial for building responsive, real-time IoT applications that require continuous two-way communication between devices and cloud platforms.

Interview Question 61: What Is LoRa and LoRaWAN?

Why This Question Is Asked: Interviewers want to check if you understand long-range communication technologies that are critical for wide-area IoT deployments.

What the Interviewer Wants to Know:

- Can you define LoRa and LoRaWAN?
- Do you know the difference between them?
- Can you explain their role in IoT systems?

How to Structure Your Answer:

1. Define LoRa and LoRaWAN simply
2. Explain how they are different
3. Mention where they are used in IoT

Sample Answer (Beginner): "LoRa stands for Long Range, and it is a way for devices to send data over long distances using very little power. LoRaWAN is a network that uses LoRa to connect many devices over a large area. In IoT, LoRa and LoRaWAN are used in smart farming, smart cities, and tracking systems."

Sample Answer (Experienced): "LoRa (Long Range) is a wireless modulation technique based on spread-spectrum technology that enables low-power, long-distance communication between IoT devices. LoRaWAN (LoRa Wide Area Network) is the communication protocol and network architecture built on top of LoRa to manage device communication, authentication, and data routing between end nodes and network servers. LoRa is the physical layer, while LoRaWAN handles the network layer and higher. They are commonly used in applications like smart agriculture, asset tracking, smart cities, and industrial monitoring where devices must operate over kilometers with minimal power consumption."

Beginner Tip: Remember: **LoRa = radio technique, LoRaWAN = network system**.

Final Thought: Understanding LoRa and LoRaWAN is vital because they make it possible to build large-scale IoT networks that are energy-efficient and cost-effective over wide geographic areas.

Interview Question 62: What Is NB-IoT?

Why This Question Is Asked: Interviewers want to check if you understand cellular-based IoT technologies that enable massive device deployments with reliable, low-power communication.

What the Interviewer Wants to Know:
- Can you define NB-IoT?
- Do you know why it is used?
- Can you explain where it fits in IoT applications?

How to Structure Your Answer:
1. Define NB-IoT simply
2. Explain its key features (low power, wide coverage)
3. Mention common use cases in IoT

Sample Answer (Beginner): "NB-IoT stands for Narrowband IoT. It is a type of wireless technology made for IoT devices that need to send small amounts of data over a long distance. It uses mobile networks like 4G but uses much less power. It is used for things like smart meters and smart parking."

Sample Answer (Experienced): "NB-IoT (Narrowband Internet of Things) is a low-power wide-area network (LPWAN) technology developed by 3GPP standards to provide long-range, energy-efficient cellular communication for IoT devices. It operates in licensed spectrum bands and offers strong indoor coverage, low device complexity, extended battery life (up to 10 years), and cost-effective deployment. NB-IoT is ideal for use cases like smart metering, asset tracking, environmental monitoring, and smart city infrastructure, where devices transmit small amounts of data infrequently but require high reliability."

Beginner Tip: Think of NB-IoT as "cellular internet" for simple, low-energy IoT devices.

Final Thought: Understanding NB-IoT is crucial because it enables large-scale IoT applications by combining the wide reach of mobile networks with the low energy demands of IoT devices.

Interview Question 63: What Is Zigbee?

Why This Question Is Asked: Interviewers want to assess if you understand short-range, low-power mesh networking technologies commonly used in IoT applications.

What the Interviewer Wants to Know:
- Can you define Zigbee?
- Do you know its key features and advantages?
- Can you explain its relevance in IoT systems?

How to Structure Your Answer:
1. Define Zigbee simply
2. Explain its characteristics (mesh networking, low power)
3. Mention common IoT applications

Sample Answer (Beginner): "Zigbee is a wireless communication technology that lets smart devices, like lights and sensors, talk to each other over short distances. It uses very little power and can create a mesh network so devices can pass messages to each other."

Sample Answer (Experienced): "Zigbee is a low-power, low-data-rate, wireless communication standard based on IEEE 802.15.4, designed for short-range device-to-device communication. It supports mesh networking, enabling devices to relay data for one another, which improves reliability and network coverage. Zigbee is widely used in IoT applications like smart home automation (e.g., smart bulbs, door locks, thermostats), industrial monitoring, and healthcare devices. Its advantages include low energy consumption, self-healing mesh capability, and scalability."

Beginner Tip: Think of Zigbee as "a team of smart devices helping each other send messages across your home."

Final Thought: Understanding Zigbee is essential because it powers many smart home and industrial IoT systems where efficient, low-power, and reliable communication is needed.

Interview Question 64: What Is Z-Wave?

Why This Question Is Asked: Interviewers want to check if you are familiar with another important low-power, short-range wireless communication technology used in IoT, especially smart homes.

What the Interviewer Wants to Know:

- Can you define Z-Wave?
- Do you understand its features and where it is used?
- Can you compare it briefly to alternatives like Zigbee?

How to Structure Your Answer:

1. Define Z-Wave simply
2. Explain its key features (mesh networking, low power, licensed frequency)
3. Mention common IoT use cases

Sample Answer (Beginner): "Z-Wave is a wireless communication technology mainly used for smart homes. It lets devices like lights, locks, and sensors talk to each other using very little power. It creates a mesh network so devices can pass messages from one to another."

Sample Answer (Experienced): "Z-Wave is a low-power, wireless communication protocol designed primarily for smart home automation. It operates in the sub-1GHz licensed radio bands (around 908 MHz in the U.S.) to reduce interference with Wi-Fi and Bluetooth. Z-Wave supports mesh networking, where each device acts as a repeater to extend coverage. It offers reliable communication, low latency, and strong interoperability between certified devices. Typical applications include smart lighting, thermostats, security systems, and door locks. Compared to Zigbee, Z-Wave has a longer range per hop but supports fewer devices in a single network."

Beginner Tip: Think of Z-Wave as "a quiet radio network just for your smart home gadgets."

Final Thought: Understanding Z-Wave is important because it is one of the major wireless standards enabling seamless and reliable communication in smart home and IoT ecosystems.

Interview Question 65: What Is BLE (Bluetooth Low Energy)?

Why This Question Is Asked: Interviewers want to assess if you understand a major wireless communication technology used for short-range, energy-efficient IoT applications.

What the Interviewer Wants to Know:

- Can you define BLE?
- Do you know its key features and benefits?
- Can you mention typical IoT use cases?

How to Structure Your Answer:

1. Define BLE simply
2. Explain its characteristics (low energy, short range)
3. Provide examples of IoT applications

Sample Answer (Beginner): "BLE stands for Bluetooth Low Energy. It's a special version of Bluetooth that uses very little power and is used to connect devices like fitness trackers, smartwatches, and wireless sensors."

Sample Answer (Experienced): "Bluetooth Low Energy (BLE) is a wireless communication protocol designed for short-range, low-power communication. Unlike classic Bluetooth, BLE focuses on minimal energy consumption while maintaining sufficient data transfer rates, making it ideal for battery-powered IoT devices. BLE is commonly used in applications like wearable fitness devices, health monitors, smart locks, and proximity beacons. It operates in the 2.4 GHz ISM band and supports mesh networking for larger deployments."

Beginner Tip: Think of BLE as "regular Bluetooth made to save battery for smart devices."

Final Thought: Understanding BLE is crucial because it powers many everyday IoT products where low energy consumption and reliable short-range communication are key.

Interview Question 66: What Is RFID and How Is It Used in IoT?

Why This Question Is Asked: Interviewers want to see if you understand a key identification technology that connects physical objects to digital systems in IoT.

What the Interviewer Wants to Know:

- Can you define RFID?
- Do you know how RFID works?
- Can you explain its role in IoT?

How to Structure Your Answer:

1. Define RFID simply
2. Explain its working principle (tags and readers)
3. Mention common IoT applications

Sample Answer (Beginner): "RFID stands for Radio-Frequency Identification. It uses radio waves to read information stored on a tag attached to an object. In IoT, RFID is used to track things like packages, inventory, or even pets."

Sample Answer (Experienced): "RFID (Radio-Frequency Identification) is a wireless technology that uses electromagnetic fields to automatically identify and track tags attached to objects. An RFID system consists of tags (which store data) and readers (which retrieve the data). RFID enables real-time object identification without direct line-of-sight, making it valuable in IoT for asset tracking, inventory management, supply chain monitoring, access control, and smart retail systems. Passive RFID tags, which do not have their own power source, are commonly used for low-cost, scalable applications."

Beginner Tip: Think of RFID as "giving everyday things a tiny radio sticker so devices can find and track them."

Final Thought: Understanding RFID is essential because it plays a crucial role in connecting the physical world to digital IoT platforms, enabling smarter logistics, security, and automation systems.

Interview Question 67: What Is NFC?

Why This Question Is Asked: Interviewers want to check if you understand Near Field Communication (NFC), a widely used short-range wireless technology in IoT and everyday applications.

What the Interviewer Wants to Know:
- Can you define NFC?
- Do you understand how it works?
- Can you give examples of its use in IoT?

How to Structure Your Answer:

1. Define NFC simply
2. Explain its characteristics (very short range, tap-to-connect)
3. Mention common use cases

Sample Answer (Beginner): "NFC stands for Near Field Communication. It allows two devices to talk to each other when they are very close—like when you tap your phone to pay at a store. In IoT, NFC is used for things like smart locks and contactless payments."

Sample Answer (Experienced): "Near Field Communication (NFC) is a short-range wireless communication technology that enables devices to exchange data over distances typically less than 10 cm. It is based on RFID technology but focuses on secure, quick, and simple two-way interactions. In IoT, NFC is used for secure device pairing, mobile payments (e.g., Apple Pay, Google Pay), access control (e.g., smart locks), identity verification, and initial device setup for smart appliances. Its low power requirements and ease of use make it ideal for applications requiring simple, quick interactions."

Beginner Tip: Think of NFC as "magic touch" technology—just bring two devices close, and they can talk to each other.

Final Thought: Understanding NFC is important because it bridges physical interactions with digital systems, enabling convenient and secure user experiences in IoT environments.

Interview Question 68: What Is GSM and How Does It Support IoT?

Why This Question Is Asked: Interviewers want to see if you understand how traditional mobile communication technologies like GSM are leveraged in IoT for connectivity over long distances.

What the Interviewer Wants to Know:

- Can you define GSM?
- Do you understand how GSM is used in IoT?
- Can you provide real-world examples?

How to Structure Your Answer:

1. Define GSM simply
2. Explain how GSM provides connectivity
3. Mention IoT use cases supported by GSM

Sample Answer (Beginner): "GSM stands for Global System for Mobile Communications. It's a mobile network technology that lets devices send messages and make calls. In IoT, GSM lets devices like GPS trackers or smart meters connect to the internet using mobile networks."

Sample Answer (Experienced): "GSM (Global System for Mobile Communications) is a standard developed to describe protocols for second-generation (2G) digital cellular networks. In IoT, GSM modules (like SIM800L) allow devices to communicate with remote servers via SMS, GPRS (General Packet Radio Service), or voice calls, providing wide-area coverage. It supports IoT use cases like asset tracking, remote monitoring, smart agriculture, and utility metering, especially where Wi-Fi or wired networks are unavailable. GSM enables reliable, low-bandwidth communication ideal for many IoT applications."

Beginner Tip: Think of GSM as "giving IoT devices a mobile phone connection to send data anywhere."

Final Thought: Understanding GSM is crucial because it provides IoT devices with an accessible, global communication network, especially for mobile and remote deployments.

Interview Question 69: What Is LTE-M?

Why This Question Is Asked: Interviewers want to check if you are familiar with modern cellular communication technologies specifically optimized for IoT applications.

What the Interviewer Wants to Know:

- Can you define LTE-M?
- Do you understand its advantages over traditional LTE and GSM?
- Can you explain where it is used in IoT?

How to Structure Your Answer:

1. Define LTE-M simply
2. Explain its key features (low power, wide coverage, mobility)
3. Mention real-world IoT applications

Sample Answer (Beginner): "LTE-M stands for LTE for Machines. It's a special version of mobile internet made for IoT devices. It uses less power and works well even when the signal is weak, like in underground parking or rural areas. It's used for things like smart meters and asset trackers."

Sample Answer (Experienced): "LTE-M (Long-Term Evolution for Machines) is a type of Low Power Wide Area Network (LPWAN) technology developed under the LTE standard, specifically for IoT applications. It offers lower power consumption, extended coverage (including deep indoor environments), reduced device complexity, and supports full mobility and voice (VoLTE). LTE-M is ideal for IoT use cases such as smart metering, fleet management, healthcare monitoring, and asset tracking, where reliable, low-latency, and mobile communication is essential. It leverages existing 4G LTE networks, ensuring wide global availability."

Beginner Tip: Think of LTE-M as "mobile internet made lighter and smarter for IoT devices."

Final Thought: Understanding LTE-M is crucial because it enables scalable, reliable, and energy-efficient IoT communication over existing cellular infrastructures, supporting both stationary and mobile IoT devices.

Interview Question 70: How Do You Secure Communication in IoT?

Why This Question Is Asked: Interviewers want to assess if you understand the critical need for securing data in transit across IoT devices, networks, and cloud platforms.

What the Interviewer Wants to Know:

- Can you explain why securing communication is important?
- Do you know methods to secure IoT communication?
- Can you provide examples of best practices?

How to Structure Your Answer:

1. Explain the need for securing communication
2. Describe methods for securing data
3. Provide real-world practices and technologies

Sample Answer (Beginner): "To secure communication in IoT, we use encryption. This means turning the data into a secret code before sending it. We also use secure networks like HTTPS and sometimes passwords or keys to make sure only trusted devices can talk to each other."

Sample Answer (Experienced): "Securing communication in IoT is essential to prevent data breaches, device hijacking, and unauthorized access. Common methods include:

- **Encryption**: Using SSL/TLS protocols to encrypt data in transit.
- **Authentication**: Ensuring only authorized devices and servers can communicate (e.g., using certificates or tokens).
- **Secure Protocols**: Using MQTT over TLS, HTTPS, or CoAP with DTLS.
- **Data Integrity Checks**: Using hashing algorithms (e.g., SHA-256) to verify data has not been tampered with.
- **VPNs and Private Networks**: Isolating IoT traffic from public internet exposure. Practical examples include using HTTPS for cloud APIs and MQTT with TLS for sensor-to-server communication."

Beginner Tip: Always "lock" your data with encryption and "check" who's talking before sharing information.

Final Thought: Understanding communication security is crucial because IoT devices often handle sensitive data and operate in environments where cyberattacks can have serious consequences.

Interview Question 71: What Is SSL/TLS?

Why This Question Is Asked: Interviewers want to check if you understand the core encryption protocols that secure IoT communication over networks like the internet.

What the Interviewer Wants to Know:

- Can you define SSL/TLS?
- Do you know how they protect communication?
- Can you give IoT-related examples?

How to Structure Your Answer:

1. Define SSL and TLS simply
2. Explain how they work (encryption and authentication)
3. Mention real-world IoT applications

Sample Answer (Beginner): "SSL and TLS are security technologies that keep data private when it travels over the internet. They create a safe, encrypted link between two devices, like a smart device and a cloud server."

Sample Answer (Experienced): "SSL (Secure Sockets Layer) and its successor TLS (Transport Layer Security) are cryptographic protocols that ensure secure communication over networks by providing encryption, authentication, and data integrity. TLS encrypts data exchanged between clients and servers, preventing eavesdropping and tampering. In IoT, SSL/TLS is used to secure MQTT connections (MQTTS), HTTPS APIs, and device-to-cloud communication to protect sensitive data and maintain trust between devices and backend systems."

Beginner Tip: Remember: TLS is the newer, safer version of SSL, and both "build a tunnel" to protect your information.

Final Thought: Understanding SSL/TLS is crucial because encrypted communication is the foundation of secure IoT systems, preventing attacks like eavesdropping and data breaches.

Interview Question 72: What Is VPN in the Context of IoT?

Why This Question Is Asked: Interviewers want to assess if you understand secure network techniques that help protect IoT devices and data in distributed environments.

What the Interviewer Wants to Know:
- Can you define a VPN?
- Do you understand its role in IoT security?
- Can you give practical examples?

How to Structure Your Answer:
1. Define VPN simply
2. Explain why VPN is important for IoT
3. Mention IoT scenarios where VPN is used

Sample Answer (Beginner): "VPN stands for Virtual Private Network. It creates a secure, private connection over the internet. In IoT, VPNs are used to protect devices by making sure their data travels safely between the device and the cloud."

Sample Answer (Experienced): "A Virtual Private Network (VPN) establishes a secure, encrypted tunnel between IoT devices and central servers over the public internet. VPNs protect data in transit from eavesdropping, ensure device-to-cloud communication privacy, and help isolate IoT devices from public network exposure. In IoT, VPNs are commonly used in smart factories, remote monitoring systems, and connected healthcare devices to safeguard critical data and maintain secure network segments."

Beginner Tip: Think of a VPN as "a secret, protected road" that only your IoT device can travel on safely.

Final Thought: Understanding VPNs is important because they help protect sensitive data, prevent unauthorized access, and enable secure remote management of IoT devices.

Interview Question 73: What Is an IoT Firewall?

Why This Question Is Asked: Interviewers want to check if you understand how network protection mechanisms are applied specifically to safeguard IoT devices and systems.

What the Interviewer Wants to Know:

- Can you define an IoT firewall?
- Do you understand how it protects devices?
- Can you give practical examples?

How to Structure Your Answer:

1. Define an IoT firewall simply
2. Explain its role (filtering traffic, blocking threats)
3. Mention real-world IoT applications

Sample Answer (Beginner): "An IoT firewall is a security tool that watches the network and blocks bad traffic from reaching IoT devices. It helps keep devices safe from hackers and harmful software."

Sample Answer (Experienced): "An IoT firewall is a specialized security solution designed to monitor, filter, and control incoming and outgoing network traffic based on security rules tailored for IoT ecosystems. Unlike traditional firewalls, IoT firewalls are optimized to handle the limited processing power and unique communication patterns of IoT devices. They help prevent unauthorized access, malware attacks, and data breaches by allowing only legitimate, trusted traffic. IoT firewalls are critical in smart homes, industrial IoT networks, and healthcare IoT environments to protect both individual devices and the overall network."

Beginner Tip: Think of an IoT firewall as "a smart security guard" that only lets safe data through to your devices.

Final Thought: Understanding IoT firewalls is important because they are one of the first lines of defense in protecting IoT systems from external cyber threats and network vulnerabilities.

Interview Question 74: What Is Network Slicing?

Why This Question Is Asked: Interviewers want to assess if you understand advanced networking techniques that are becoming important for supporting diverse IoT applications on 5G networks.

What the Interviewer Wants to Know:

- Can you define network slicing?
- Do you understand why it's important for IoT?
- Can you give real-world examples?

How to Structure Your Answer:

1. Define network slicing simply
2. Explain how it works (separate "slices" for different needs)
3. Mention practical IoT applications

Sample Answer (Beginner): "Network slicing means dividing a big network into smaller, separate networks. Each small network is made for a special job, like controlling smart cars or running smart factories."

Sample Answer (Experienced): "Network slicing is a 5G networking technique that creates multiple virtual networks (or "slices") on a shared physical network infrastructure. Each slice is optimized to meet the specific requirements of different applications—such as low latency for autonomous vehicles, high bandwidth for video surveillance, or energy efficiency for massive IoT deployments. In IoT, network slicing allows service providers to deliver customized, reliable, and secure network services for critical use cases like smart cities, remote healthcare, and industrial automation."

Beginner Tip: Think of network slicing as "giving each IoT service its own private lane on a busy internet highway."

Final Thought: Understanding network slicing is important because it allows networks to efficiently support the diverse needs of different IoT applications with varying speed, reliability, and security requirements.

Interview Question 75: What Are the Bandwidth Requirements for IoT?

Why This Question Is Asked: Interviewers want to check if you understand how different IoT applications have varying network bandwidth needs depending on their use case.

What the Interviewer Wants to Know:

- Can you explain bandwidth in simple terms?
- Do you know how bandwidth needs vary across IoT systems?
- Can you give examples of low vs. high bandwidth IoT applications?

How to Structure Your Answer:

1. Define bandwidth simply
2. Explain factors affecting IoT bandwidth needs
3. Provide examples of different IoT applications

Sample Answer (Beginner): "Bandwidth is how much data can move through a network at one time. Some IoT devices, like temperature sensors, need very little bandwidth. Other devices, like security cameras, need a lot more because they send big video files."

Sample Answer (Experienced): "Bandwidth refers to the maximum rate at which data can be transferred over a network connection, typically measured in bits per second (bps). In IoT, bandwidth requirements vary widely depending on the application:

- **Low-bandwidth IoT devices**: Environmental sensors, smart meters, and wearables typically transmit small, infrequent data packets and can operate on low-bandwidth networks like NB-IoT or LoRaWAN.
- **High-bandwidth IoT devices**: Video surveillance systems, industrial automation systems with real-time analytics, and smart city infrastructures often require higher bandwidth connections like LTE-M, 5G, or Wi-Fi 6. Factors affecting bandwidth needs

include data size, transmission frequency, real-time requirements, and number of connected devices."

Beginner Tip: Imagine bandwidth like "a road" — small IoT devices only need a bicycle lane, but video cameras need a whole highway.

Final Thought: Understanding bandwidth requirements is important because choosing the right network technology ensures IoT applications are reliable, efficient, and cost-effective.

Section 4: Platforms, Cloud & Security (76–90)

Interview Question 76: What Are IoT Platforms?

Why This Question Is Asked: Interviewers want to check if you understand the software and service ecosystems that support IoT device management, data collection, and application development.

What the Interviewer Wants to Know:

- Can you define what an IoT platform is?
- Do you understand its key functions?
- Can you give examples of popular IoT platforms?

How to Structure Your Answer:

1. Define an IoT platform simply
2. Explain the main functions (device management, data analytics, connectivity)
3. Mention examples of platforms

Sample Answer (Beginner): "An IoT platform is a system that helps connect, manage, and control smart devices. It also collects their data and helps apps use it. Examples include AWS IoT and Google Cloud IoT."

Sample Answer (Experienced): "An IoT platform is a cloud-based or on-premise service that provides the tools and infrastructure to connect, manage, secure, and analyze IoT devices and their data. Core functionalities include device provisioning, remote management, data collection, analytics, application enablement, and integration with cloud services. Examples of popular IoT platforms include AWS IoT Core, Microsoft Azure IoT Hub, Google Cloud IoT, IBM Watson IoT, and open-source platforms like ThingsBoard. IoT platforms help developers quickly build scalable, secure, and feature-rich IoT solutions."

Beginner Tip: Think of an IoT platform as "the control center" that keeps all your smart devices connected and working together.

Final Thought: Understanding IoT platforms is critical because they are the backbone that enables easy device communication, large-scale deployment, and smart data-driven applications in IoT ecosystems.

Interview Question 76: What Are IoT Platforms?

Why This Question Is Asked: Interviewers want to check if you understand the software and service ecosystems that support IoT device management, data collection, and application development.

What the Interviewer Wants to Know:
- Can you define what an IoT platform is?
- Do you understand its key functions?
- Can you give examples of popular IoT platforms?

How to Structure Your Answer:
1. Define an IoT platform simply
2. Explain the main functions (device management, data analytics, connectivity)
3. Mention examples of platforms

Sample Answer (Beginner): "An IoT platform is a system that helps connect, manage, and control smart devices. It also collects their data and helps apps use it. Examples include AWS IoT and Google Cloud IoT."

Sample Answer (Experienced): "An IoT platform is a cloud-based or on-premise service that provides the tools and infrastructure to connect, manage, secure, and analyze IoT devices and their data. Core functionalities include device provisioning, remote management, data collection, analytics, application enablement, and integration with cloud services. Examples of popular IoT platforms include AWS IoT Core, Microsoft Azure IoT Hub, Google Cloud IoT, IBM Watson IoT, ThingsBoard, Cisco IoT Cloud Connect, and Oracle IoT Cloud. IoT platforms help developers quickly build scalable, secure, and feature-rich IoT solutions."

Beginner Tip: Think of an IoT platform as "the control center" that keeps all your smart devices connected and working together.

Final Thought: Understanding IoT platforms is critical because they are the backbone that enables easy device communication, large-scale deployment, and smart data-driven applications in IoT ecosystems.

Interview Question 77: Name Some Popular IoT Platforms

Why This Question Is Asked: Interviewers want to assess if you are familiar with major industry-standard tools that are widely used to deploy and manage IoT solutions.

What the Interviewer Wants to Know:

- Can you name key IoT platforms?
- Do you know what they are commonly used for?

How to Structure Your Answer:

1. List popular IoT platforms
2. Briefly mention what they offer
3. Optionally categorize them by type (cloud-based, open-source, etc.)

Sample Answer (Beginner): "Some popular IoT platforms are AWS IoT Core, Microsoft Azure IoT Hub, and Google Cloud IoT. These platforms help manage smart devices, collect their data, and keep them connected."

Sample Answer (Experienced): "Popular IoT platforms include:

- **AWS IoT Core**: Provides secure device connectivity, data processing, and cloud integration.
- **Microsoft Azure IoT Hub**: Offers device management, bi-directional communication, and analytics tools.
- **Google Cloud IoT Core**: Supports scalable device connection and big data analysis.

- **IBM Watson IoT**: Focuses on cognitive computing and AI integration with IoT data.
- **ThingsBoard**: An open-source platform for device management, data collection, and visualization.
- **Particle**: Provides a full-stack platform for IoT prototyping and deployment.
- **Siemens MindSphere**: Specializes in industrial IoT for manufacturing and infrastructure. Each platform provides tools for secure communication, remote device management, real-time analytics, and application development."

Beginner Tip: Start by learning one major platform (like AWS or Azure) to understand the basic services and workflow.

Final Thought: Knowing popular IoT platforms is important because they form the backbone for designing scalable, secure, and efficient IoT solutions across industries.

Interview Question 78: What Is Blynk and How Is It Used?

Why This Question Is Asked: Interviewers want to assess if you are familiar with user-friendly IoT platforms that simplify app development and device control.

What the Interviewer Wants to Know:

- Can you define what Blynk is?
- Do you understand its key features?
- Can you explain how it is used in IoT projects?

How to Structure Your Answer:

1. Define Blynk simply
2. Explain its key features (mobile apps, device control, cloud services)
3. Provide real-world IoT use examples

Sample Answer (Beginner): "Blynk is a platform that lets you easily build apps to control IoT devices from your phone. You can use it to turn on lights, check sensors, or monitor your devices anywhere."

Sample Answer (Experienced): "Blynk is a low-code IoT platform that enables developers to quickly create mobile and web applications to control and monitor IoT devices. It provides a mobile app builder, a cloud server for device management, and a device firmware library. Developers can connect devices like Arduino, ESP32, Raspberry Pi, and more to Blynk and create custom dashboards without heavy coding. Blynk is widely used in DIY projects, smart home automation, and rapid IoT prototyping because of its ease of use, real-time control, and cross-platform support."

Beginner Tip: Think of Blynk as "the easiest way to make your own app to control smart gadgets."

Final Thought: Understanding Blynk is important because it empowers developers and hobbyists to build practical IoT solutions quickly without deep mobile app development skills.

Interview Question 79: What Is Node-RED?

Why This Question Is Asked: Interviewers want to see if you know about popular tools that simplify the design of IoT workflows and applications without heavy coding.

What the Interviewer Wants to Know:

- Can you define Node-RED?
- Do you understand its role in IoT application development?
- Can you provide practical use cases?

How to Structure Your Answer:

1. Define Node-RED simply
2. Explain its key features (visual programming, easy device integration)
3. Mention real-world examples

Sample Answer (Beginner): "Node-RED is a tool that lets you build smart projects by connecting blocks together without needing a lot of coding. It's like making a flowchart that controls your IoT devices."

Sample Answer (Experienced): "Node-RED is a flow-based, low-code programming tool developed by IBM for wiring together devices, APIs, and services in IoT and web applications. It uses a browser-based visual editor where users create flows by connecting nodes that represent different functions, inputs, outputs, and services. Node-RED simplifies IoT integration by supporting protocols like MQTT, HTTP, and WebSocket, and is widely used for data collection, automation, and building dashboards. It's ideal for rapid prototyping and deploying complex IoT logic without writing extensive code."

Beginner Tip: Think of Node-RED as "a visual puzzle board where you connect smart pieces to build your IoT system."

Final Thought: Understanding Node-RED is important because it makes IoT development faster, easier, and more accessible for both beginners and experienced developers.

Interview Question 80: What Is AWS IoT Core?

Why This Question Is Asked: Interviewers want to assess if you are familiar with major cloud-based IoT solutions that help in securely connecting and managing IoT devices at scale.

What the Interviewer Wants to Know:

- Can you define AWS IoT Core?
- Do you understand its key functions and benefits?
- Can you explain how it is used in IoT solutions?

How to Structure Your Answer:

1. Define AWS IoT Core simply
2. Explain its key features (connectivity, security, device management)
3. Provide practical use cases

Sample Answer (Beginner): "AWS IoT Core is a cloud service from Amazon that helps connect smart devices to the internet and manage them. It lets devices talk to each other and to apps safely and easily."

Sample Answer (Experienced): "AWS IoT Core is a managed cloud service by Amazon Web Services that enables secure, scalable, and low-latency communication between IoT devices and cloud applications. It supports device authentication, message brokering (using MQTT, HTTP, and WebSocket protocols), real-time data processing, and integration with other AWS services like Lambda, DynamoDB, and S3 for advanced analytics and automation. AWS IoT Core is widely used in applications like industrial automation, smart home ecosystems, predictive maintenance, and fleet management."

Beginner Tip: Think of AWS IoT Core as "the brain in the cloud" that connects, talks to, and manages all your IoT devices.

Final Thought: Understanding AWS IoT Core is important because it enables you to build scalable, secure, and intelligent IoT solutions without having to manage complex server infrastructures yourself.

Interview Question 80: What Is AWS IoT Core?

Why This Question Is Asked: Interviewers want to assess if you are familiar with major cloud-based IoT solutions that help in securely connecting and managing IoT devices at scale.

What the Interviewer Wants to Know:

- Can you define AWS IoT Core?
- Do you understand its key functions and benefits?
- Can you explain how it is used in IoT solutions?

How to Structure Your Answer:

1. Define AWS IoT Core simply
2. Explain its key features (connectivity, security, device management)
3. Provide practical use cases

Sample Answer (Beginner): "AWS IoT Core is a cloud service from Amazon that helps connect smart devices to the internet and manage them. It lets devices talk to each other and to apps safely and easily."

Sample Answer (Experienced): "AWS IoT Core is a managed cloud service by Amazon Web Services that enables secure, scalable, and low-latency communication between IoT devices and cloud applications. It supports device authentication, message brokering (using MQTT, HTTP, and WebSocket protocols), real-time data processing, and integration with other AWS services like Lambda, DynamoDB, and S3 for advanced analytics and automation. AWS IoT Core is widely used in applications like industrial automation, smart home ecosystems, predictive maintenance, and fleet management."

Beginner Tip: Think of AWS IoT Core as "the brain in the cloud" that connects, talks to, and manages all your IoT devices.

Final Thought: Understanding AWS IoT Core is important because it enables you to build scalable, secure, and intelligent IoT solutions without having to manage complex server infrastructures yourself.

Interview Question 81: What Is ThingSpeak?

Why This Question Is Asked: Interviewers want to assess if you are familiar with simple, open-source IoT platforms used for quick data collection, visualization, and analysis.

What the Interviewer Wants to Know:

- Can you define ThingSpeak?
- Do you understand its main features?
- Can you explain its role in IoT projects?

How to Structure Your Answer:

1. Define ThingSpeak simply
2. Explain its key capabilities (data collection, visualization, analysis)
3. Mention practical IoT use cases

Sample Answer (Beginner): "ThingSpeak is a website where IoT devices can send their data, like temperature readings, and you can see that data on graphs. It's useful for making simple smart projects."

Sample Answer (Experienced): "ThingSpeak is an open-source IoT platform that allows devices to send data to the cloud using HTTP or MQTT protocols. It provides easy-to-use tools for real-time data collection, visualization, and basic analytics. ThingSpeak is often used for prototyping IoT solutions, academic research, environmental monitoring, and home automation projects. It also integrates with MATLAB for advanced data analysis and predictive modeling."

Beginner Tip: Think of ThingSpeak as "a cloud notebook" where your devices can write down their sensor readings and draw simple charts.

Final Thought: Understanding ThingSpeak is useful because it provides a beginner-friendly, fast, and free way to visualize and analyze IoT data without needing complex server setups.

Interview Question 82: What Is Google Cloud IoT?

Why This Question Is Asked: Interviewers want to see if you understand major cloud solutions that support the deployment, management, and scaling of IoT devices and applications.

What the Interviewer Wants to Know:
- Can you define Google Cloud IoT?
- Do you understand its features and services?
- Can you explain how it fits into IoT solutions?

How to Structure Your Answer:
1. Define Google Cloud IoT simply
2. Explain its key features (device management, data collection, analytics)
3. Mention practical IoT applications

Sample Answer (Beginner): "Google Cloud IoT is a service that helps connect smart devices to Google's cloud. It collects data from those devices and lets you see or analyze that data."

Sample Answer (Experienced): "Google Cloud IoT is a suite of managed services that allows for secure device connection, management, data ingestion, and analytics using Google's cloud infrastructure. Key components include Cloud IoT Core (for device connectivity), Cloud Pub/Sub (for messaging), BigQuery (for large-scale data analysis), and Cloud Functions (for event-driven serverless computing). It is widely used in smart city projects, industrial monitoring, predictive maintenance, and energy management solutions."

Beginner Tip: Think of Google Cloud IoT as "Google's smart hub in the cloud" where all your IoT devices send their information to be stored, managed, and analyzed.

Final Thought: Understanding Google Cloud IoT is important because it offers scalable, secure, and powerful tools for building complex IoT ecosystems integrated with advanced machine learning and data analytics capabilities.

Interview Question 83: What Is Microsoft Azure IoT?

Why This Question Is Asked: Interviewers want to check if you are familiar with one of the leading enterprise-grade platforms for building, connecting, and managing IoT solutions.

What the Interviewer Wants to Know:

- Can you define Microsoft Azure IoT?
- Do you understand its main components and services?
- Can you explain how it is used in IoT deployments?

How to Structure Your Answer:

1. Define Microsoft Azure IoT simply
2. Highlight its core services (IoT Hub, IoT Central, Edge computing)
3. Provide real-world application examples

Sample Answer (Beginner): "Microsoft Azure IoT is a cloud service that helps you connect, monitor, and manage smart devices. It gives tools to build and run IoT projects easily."

Sample Answer (Experienced): "Microsoft Azure IoT is a suite of cloud services offered by Microsoft for connecting, managing, and analyzing IoT devices and data. Core components include Azure IoT Hub (secure device-to-cloud communication), Azure IoT Central (low-code platform for IoT applications), and Azure IoT Edge (edge computing services). It also offers integration with Azure Machine Learning, Stream Analytics, and Digital Twins for advanced insights and automation. Azure IoT is used across industries such as smart cities, manufacturing, healthcare, and agriculture."

Beginner Tip: Think of Microsoft Azure IoT as "a giant cloud toolbox" that helps manage, monitor, and automate lots of IoT devices at once.

Final Thought: Understanding Microsoft Azure IoT is important because it provides scalable, secure, and intelligent infrastructure for building real-world IoT solutions across various industries.

Interview Question 84: What Is Real-Time Analytics?

Why This Question Is Asked: Interviewers want to assess if you understand how IoT systems can process and act on data instantly, which is critical for many smart applications.

What the Interviewer Wants to Know:

- Can you define real-time analytics?
- Do you understand why it's important in IoT?
- Can you provide examples where real-time analytics is used?

How to Structure Your Answer:

1. Define real-time analytics simply
2. Explain why it matters
3. Give examples of real-time IoT applications

Sample Answer (Beginner): "Real-time analytics means looking at data and getting useful information from it right away, without waiting. In IoT, it's used for things like alerting when a machine is overheating."

Sample Answer (Experienced): "Real-time analytics refers to the immediate processing and analysis of data as it is generated, enabling instant insights and actions. In IoT systems, real-time analytics is critical for applications that require immediate response, such as industrial monitoring, predictive maintenance, smart traffic control, and healthcare monitoring. It allows organizations to detect anomalies, trigger alarms, optimize operations, and enhance decision-making instantly based on live sensor data."

Beginner Tip: Think of real-time analytics as "listening to your smart devices and reacting right away when something important happens."

Final Thought: Understanding real-time analytics is essential because many IoT applications depend on immediate data-driven decisions to ensure safety, efficiency, and reliability.

Interview Question 85: How Does IoT Integrate with Cloud Computing?

Why This Question Is Asked: Interviewers want to assess if you understand the relationship between IoT devices and cloud infrastructure, which is crucial for scalable, efficient systems.

What the Interviewer Wants to Know:

- Can you explain the integration between IoT and cloud?
- Do you know the benefits and workflows involved?
- Can you provide examples of cloud-based IoT systems?

How to Structure Your Answer:

1. Describe how IoT and cloud work together
2. Explain the benefits of using the cloud
3. Give real-world application examples

Sample Answer (Beginner): "IoT devices collect data and send it to the cloud, where the data is stored and analyzed. The cloud also helps control devices remotely. For example, a smart thermostat sends temperature data to the cloud, and you can change the setting using a mobile app."

Sample Answer (Experienced): "IoT devices integrate with cloud computing by transmitting collected data to cloud platforms where it is stored, processed, analyzed, and visualized. The cloud provides scalable infrastructure, real-time analytics, device management, security, and application hosting. Benefits include reduced local storage needs, centralized control, remote access, and the ability to leverage advanced services like machine learning. Examples include smart city traffic systems using AWS IoT Core, industrial IoT platforms running on Azure IoT Hub, and healthcare monitoring devices leveraging Google Cloud IoT."

Beginner Tip: Think of cloud computing as "the brain" that helps IoT devices store, understand, and act on the information they collect.

Final Thought: Understanding IoT-cloud integration is crucial because it enables building powerful, flexible, and intelligent IoT systems that are easy to scale and manage.

Interview Question 86: What Are the Types of Data Storage in IoT?

Why This Question Is Asked: Interviewers want to check if you understand the different methods available for storing massive amounts of IoT-generated data efficiently and securely.

What the Interviewer Wants to Know:
- Can you name and explain storage types?
- Do you understand when each type is used?
- Can you provide examples?

How to Structure Your Answer:
1. List the main types of data storage
2. Briefly explain each type
3. Mention examples of IoT use cases for each

Sample Answer (Beginner): "In IoT, data can be stored on the device itself (local storage) or sent to the cloud (cloud storage). Sometimes devices store a little bit first and then send it when they have a good connection."

Sample Answer (Experienced): "The main types of data storage in IoT are:

- **Local Storage**: Data is stored directly on the device or a nearby gateway. Used when immediate cloud connectivity is unavailable (e.g., industrial sensors in remote areas).
- **Cloud Storage**: Data is sent and stored on remote cloud servers (e.g., AWS S3, Azure Blob Storage), ideal for large-scale storage and analytics.
- **Edge Storage**: Data is processed and temporarily stored at the network edge (e.g., on IoT gateways) to reduce latency before selective data is sent to the cloud.
- **Hybrid Storage**: A combination of local, edge, and cloud storage depending on real-time needs and system design. Examples include local SD cards in weather stations, edge servers in smart factories, and cloud-based databases for smart home ecosystems."

Beginner Tip: Think of local storage as "keeping notes on your desk," cloud storage as "saving to Google Drive," and edge storage as "sorting important notes nearby before sending to the cloud."

Final Thought: Understanding data storage types is important because choosing the right method affects system performance, cost, and reliability in IoT solutions.

Interview Question 87: What Is OTA (Over-The-Air) Firmware Update?

Why This Question Is Asked: Interviewers want to see if you understand how remote device management works, especially when updating firmware without physical access to IoT devices.

What the Interviewer Wants to Know:
- Can you define OTA updates?
- Do you understand how they are important for IoT systems?
- Can you explain practical applications?

How to Structure Your Answer:
1. Define OTA simply
2. Explain why it is important
3. Give examples of OTA use in IoT

Sample Answer (Beginner): "OTA means sending a software update to a device over the internet, so you don't have to go and update it by hand. In IoT, it's used to fix bugs or add new features to devices like smart thermostats or security cameras."

Sample Answer (Experienced): "OTA (Over-The-Air) firmware update refers to the process of remotely updating the software or firmware of an IoT device over a wireless network. It enables bug fixes, security patches, feature upgrades, and system optimizations without physical device access. OTA is critical in IoT for maintaining device security, enhancing functionality, and reducing maintenance costs. Practical applications include updating software on smart home hubs, wearable devices, automotive control systems, and industrial sensors."

Beginner Tip: Think of OTA like "sending a remote upgrade to your smart gadget, just like updating apps on your phone without plugging it in."

Final Thought: Understanding OTA updates is essential because it ensures that IoT devices stay secure, up-to-date, and functional throughout their lifecycle with minimal effort.

Interview Question 88: How Is Data Encryption Handled in IoT?

Why This Question Is Asked: Interviewers want to assess if you understand one of the key security techniques used to protect sensitive data traveling between IoT devices and systems.

What the Interviewer Wants to Know:

- Can you define data encryption in IoT?
- Do you understand common encryption methods?
- Can you explain why encryption is critical for IoT?

How to Structure Your Answer:

1. Define data encryption simply
2. Explain how it works in IoT
3. Give examples of encryption technologies and practices

Sample Answer (Beginner): "Data encryption in IoT means turning the information into a secret code before sending it. This way, if hackers catch the data, they can't understand it. It's like locking the data with a password."

Sample Answer (Experienced): "Data encryption in IoT involves converting readable data (plaintext) into an unreadable format (ciphertext) to prevent unauthorized access during transmission or storage. Common encryption techniques include symmetric encryption (e.g., AES) for device-to-device communication and asymmetric encryption (e.g., RSA) for secure key exchange. Protocols like SSL/TLS are widely used to secure data in transit. End-to-end encryption and lightweight encryption algorithms are often applied to fit the resource constraints of IoT devices. Proper encryption is critical to protect sensitive data such as user information, telemetry, and control signals in IoT systems."

Beginner Tip: Imagine encryption as "locking a message in a special box that only the right key can open."

Final Thought: Understanding data encryption is essential because strong encryption practices are the foundation of securing IoT systems against cyber threats and ensuring data privacy and integrity.

Interview Question 89: What Is Device Authentication?

Why This Question Is Asked: Interviewers want to assess if you understand how IoT systems verify the identity of devices before allowing communication or data exchange.

What the Interviewer Wants to Know:

- Can you define device authentication?
- Do you understand how it protects IoT networks?
- Can you give examples of authentication methods?

How to Structure Your Answer:

1. Define device authentication simply
2. Explain why it is important in IoT
3. Mention common methods used

Sample Answer (Beginner): "Device authentication means checking if a device is really the one it says it is before letting it join the network. It's like showing your ID before you enter a secure building."

Sample Answer (Experienced): "Device authentication is the process of verifying the identity of an IoT device before allowing it to connect to a network or service. This ensures that only trusted, authorized devices can communicate within the IoT system. Common methods include pre-shared keys, digital certificates (X.509), OAuth tokens, and secure boot mechanisms. Device authentication prevents unauthorized access, protects against impersonation attacks, and helps maintain the integrity of the entire IoT ecosystem."

Beginner Tip: Think of device authentication as "checking the ID card of every device before letting it join the club."

Final Thought: Understanding device authentication is crucial because it forms the first line of defense in securing IoT networks and ensuring that only trusted devices can access and exchange data.

Interview Question 90: What Are Common IoT Security Vulnerabilities?

Why This Question Is Asked: Interviewers want to assess if you understand the typical security risks that can affect IoT systems and how these weaknesses can be mitigated.

What the Interviewer Wants to Know:

- Can you identify major vulnerabilities in IoT systems?
- Do you understand how these vulnerabilities can be exploited?
- Can you mention examples or mitigation strategies?

How to Structure Your Answer:

1. List common IoT security vulnerabilities
2. Briefly explain why they are dangerous
3. Mention examples or mitigation practices

Sample Answer (Beginner): "Some common IoT security problems are weak passwords, outdated software, and sending data without encryption. These problems make it easier for hackers to break into devices."

Sample Answer (Experienced): "Common IoT security vulnerabilities include:

- **Weak or Default Credentials**: Devices shipped with easily guessable usernames and passwords.
- **Unencrypted Data Transmission**: Sensitive data sent without encryption, making it vulnerable to interception.
- **Outdated Firmware**: Lack of regular updates exposes devices to known exploits.
- **Poor Device Authentication**: Weak identity verification can allow unauthorized devices to join networks.
- **Insecure APIs**: Poorly secured application interfaces can leak or expose device data.
- **Lack of Physical Security**: Physical access to IoT devices can allow tampering or data extraction. Mitigation includes strong authentication, regular OTA updates, encryption (SSL/TLS), secure coding practices, and network segmentation."

Beginner Tip: Imagine IoT security like "locking your doors, updating your alarm system, and making sure only trusted people have the keys."

Final Thought: Understanding IoT vulnerabilities is critical because securing even small devices helps protect the entire system from large-scale cyberattacks and breaches.

Section 5: Real-World Scenarios & Projects (91–101)

Interview Question 91: How Would You Build a Smart Home System?

Why This Question Is Asked: Interviewers want to assess if you can plan, design, and integrate different IoT components into a functional, real-world system.

What the Interviewer Wants to Know:

- Can you describe a clear, structured approach?
- Do you know what devices, platforms, and protocols to use?
- Can you think about security, scalability, and user experience?

How to Structure Your Answer:

1. Briefly explain the planning phase
2. List key components needed
3. Outline how the system would be integrated and secured

Sample Answer (Beginner): "First, I would decide what smart devices I want, like smart lights, a thermostat, and security cameras. Then I would use a hub or platform, like Google Home or Amazon Alexa, to connect everything. I'd make sure to use Wi-Fi or Zigbee for communication and add passwords to keep the system secure."

Sample Answer (Experienced): "To build a smart home system, I would:

1. **Identify Requirements**: Define goals like security, energy efficiency, and convenience.
2. **Select Devices**: Choose smart lights, thermostats, locks, cameras, sensors, and voice assistants.
3. **Select a Central Platform**: Use platforms like Google Home, Apple HomeKit, Amazon Alexa, or open-source solutions like Home Assistant.

4. **Connectivity and Protocols**: Ensure devices support Wi-Fi, Zigbee, Z-Wave, or Bluetooth Low Energy (BLE).
5. **Integration**: Use a central hub to automate scenes and routines.
6. **Security**: Implement network segmentation (VLANs for IoT), strong passwords, two-factor authentication, and OTA updates.
7. **Cloud and Local Storage**: Use cloud for remote access but prefer local storage for sensitive video footage when possible.
8. **Testing and Optimization**: Fine-tune automations and monitor device health regularly. Example: Setting up a smart home where the door unlocks automatically via NFC tag, lights adjust based on presence, and thermostats optimize heating schedules."

Beginner Tip: Start simple—connect a few lights and sensors first, then add more smart devices step-by-step.

Final Thought: Knowing how to design and build a smart home system shows that you can integrate hardware, software, networking, and security into a practical IoT solution.

Interview Question 92: How Do You Create a Weather Monitoring System?

Why This Question Is Asked: Interviewers want to check if you can design a practical IoT project that collects, processes, and displays real-world environmental data.

What the Interviewer Wants to Know:

- Can you outline a step-by-step approach?
- Do you know what sensors, microcontrollers, and platforms to use?
- Can you mention how to collect, store, and visualize the data?

How to Structure Your Answer:

1. Briefly describe the system goal
2. List the components needed
3. Outline the workflow: sensing, communication, storage, visualization

Sample Answer (Beginner): "First, I would use sensors to measure temperature, humidity, and pressure. I'd connect them to a microcontroller like Arduino or ESP32. Then I would send the data to a cloud platform like ThingSpeak, where I could see graphs of the weather data."

Sample Answer (Experienced): "To create a weather monitoring system, I would:

1. **Select Sensors**: Use DHT22 (temperature and humidity), BMP280 (pressure), and a rain gauge.
2. **Choose a Microcontroller**: ESP32 for built-in Wi-Fi and low-power operation.
3. **Connectivity**: Connect the sensors to the ESP32, and program it to send data at intervals.
4. **Data Transmission**: Use MQTT or HTTP to send data to a cloud platform (e.g., AWS IoT, ThingSpeak, or Google Cloud IoT).
5. **Data Storage**: Store the collected data in cloud databases (e.g., AWS DynamoDB, Google Cloud Storage).
6. **Visualization**: Use dashboards (e.g., Grafana, ThingSpeak charts) for real-time weather monitoring.
7. **Optional**: Add local display with an OLED screen for immediate readings.
8. **Security Measures**: Implement SSL/TLS encryption for data transmission and secure device authentication. Example: A solar-powered weather station in a field sending temperature, humidity, and rainfall data every 10 minutes to a live dashboard."

Beginner Tip: Start simple—measure temperature and humidity first, then expand with more sensors later.

Final Thought: Designing a weather monitoring system shows your ability to connect sensors, program devices, handle cloud communication, and build real-world IoT solutions with visualization and analytics.

Interview Question 93: Describe a Smart Irrigation Project Using IoT

Why This Question Is Asked: Interviewers want to evaluate your ability to design an IoT solution that addresses a real-world problem, combining sensors, automation, and connectivity.

What the Interviewer Wants to Know:

- Can you describe the key components and workflow?
- Do you understand how to optimize resources like water and energy?
- Can you highlight practical benefits?

How to Structure Your Answer:

1. Briefly describe the project goal
2. List the components used
3. Explain the workflow: sensing, decision-making, and action

Sample Answer (Beginner): "A smart irrigation system uses soil moisture sensors to check if plants need water. If the soil is dry, a smart controller turns on the water. It can also connect to the internet to adjust watering based on the weather."

Sample Answer (Experienced): "A smart irrigation project involves:

1. **Sensors**: Soil moisture sensors, temperature sensors, and rain sensors.
2. **Microcontroller**: ESP32 or Arduino to collect sensor data.
3. **Connectivity**: Wi-Fi, LoRa, or NB-IoT to send data to a cloud platform.
4. **Cloud Services**: AWS IoT or Google Cloud IoT to store data and apply decision-making logic.

5. **Control System**: Solenoid valves controlled via relays based on sensor thresholds or predictive weather models.
6. **Automation**: The system automatically waters plants when soil moisture is low and pauses watering if rain is detected or forecasted.
7. **Dashboard**: Visualize soil and weather conditions and remotely control irrigation through a web or mobile app.
8. **Security**: Encrypt communications and authenticate devices to prevent unauthorized control. Example: A smart farm where irrigation is optimized daily based on soil data and weather forecasts, reducing water consumption by 30%."

Beginner Tip: Focus first on automating basic moisture-based watering before adding advanced weather prediction features.

Final Thought: Building a smart irrigation system shows your ability to apply IoT to conserve resources, automate decisions, and improve agricultural efficiency through real-time monitoring and control.

Interview Question 94: What Is Predictive Maintenance in IoT?

Why This Question Is Asked: Interviewers want to assess if you understand how IoT enables smarter maintenance strategies to prevent equipment failure and reduce operational costs.

What the Interviewer Wants to Know:

- Can you define predictive maintenance?
- Do you understand how IoT helps enable it?
- Can you provide practical examples?

How to Structure Your Answer:

1. Define predictive maintenance simply
2. Explain the IoT technologies involved
3. Give real-world examples

Sample Answer (Beginner): "Predictive maintenance means using sensors to watch machines and find problems before they break. This way, repairs can be done early and save money."

Sample Answer (Experienced): "Predictive maintenance in IoT refers to the use of real-time sensor data, machine learning models, and cloud analytics to predict when equipment will require maintenance before a failure occurs. IoT devices monitor key parameters like vibration, temperature, or pressure. Data is analyzed to identify patterns that signal wear or malfunction. Applications include manufacturing machinery, elevators, wind turbines, and vehicles. Predictive maintenance reduces downtime, extends equipment life, and optimizes maintenance schedules."

Beginner Tip: Think of predictive maintenance like "getting a warning from your car before it breaks down, based on what the sensors detect."

Final Thought: Understanding predictive maintenance is essential because it shows how IoT adds real business value by making operations safer, more efficient, and cost-effective through proactive strategies.

Interview Question 95: How Is IoT Used in Smart Cities?

Why This Question Is Asked: Interviewers want to evaluate if you understand how IoT technologies are applied at a large scale to improve urban living, resource management, and public services.

What the Interviewer Wants to Know:

- Can you describe IoT applications in smart cities?
- Do you understand the benefits for governments and citizens?
- Can you give real-world examples?

How to Structure Your Answer:

1. Define smart cities and IoT's role
2. List major IoT applications in smart cities
3. Provide practical examples

Sample Answer (Beginner): "IoT helps make cities smarter by using sensors to manage traffic, monitor air quality, save energy with smart lights, and make things work better for people."

Sample Answer (Experienced): "IoT in smart cities involves connecting sensors, devices, and systems to collect and analyze data that improves urban living. Key applications include:

- **Smart Traffic Management**: Sensors monitor traffic flow and optimize signals to reduce congestion.
- **Smart Lighting**: Streetlights adjust brightness based on activity or time of day to save energy.
- **Waste Management**: Smart bins signal when they are full, improving collection routes.
- **Environmental Monitoring**: Air quality, noise, and water sensors help manage pollution.
- **Public Safety**: IoT-enabled surveillance and emergency response systems improve safety.
- **Smart Parking**: Sensors guide drivers to available parking spots. Examples include Barcelona's smart lighting and parking systems and Singapore's smart traffic solutions."

Beginner Tip: Think of a smart city as "a city that listens to sensors and adjusts itself to make life easier and safer for people."

Final Thought: Understanding IoT's role in smart cities shows that you can envision scalable, real-world IoT applications that tackle big challenges like traffic, pollution, energy waste, and public safety.

Interview Question 96: How Is IoT Transforming the Healthcare Industry?

Why This Question Is Asked: Interviewers want to assess if you understand how IoT innovations are reshaping healthcare services, patient monitoring, and medical operations.

What the Interviewer Wants to Know:

- Can you describe IoT applications in healthcare?
- Do you understand the impact on patients, doctors, and hospitals?
- Can you give real-world examples?

How to Structure Your Answer:

1. Briefly explain IoT's role in healthcare
2. List key IoT applications
3. Provide examples and benefits

Sample Answer (Beginner): "IoT helps doctors and patients by using smart devices like health monitors and trackers. It makes it easier to check health problems early and take care of patients better."

Sample Answer (Experienced): "IoT is transforming healthcare by enabling continuous patient monitoring, real-time data collection, remote diagnosis, and improved operational efficiency. Key applications include:

- **Wearable Health Devices**: Track heart rate, blood pressure, glucose levels, and send alerts for abnormalities.
- **Remote Patient Monitoring**: IoT devices monitor chronic conditions at home, reducing hospital visits.
- **Smart Hospitals**: IoT-enabled equipment and asset tracking improve hospital management.
- **Connected Inhalers and Smart Pills**: Ensure medication adherence and track treatment effectiveness.
- **Emergency Response Systems**: IoT wearables can automatically alert emergency services if a patient collapses. Examples include

Fitbit for fitness tracking, continuous glucose monitors for diabetics, and remote monitoring platforms used in telemedicine."

Beginner Tip: Think of IoT in healthcare as "giving doctors extra eyes and tools to take better care of patients, even from far away."

Final Thought: Understanding IoT in healthcare shows that you recognize how technology can improve patient outcomes, lower costs, and make healthcare more proactive and accessible.

Interview Question 97: How Would You Track a Vehicle Using GPS and IoT?

Why This Question Is Asked: Interviewers want to evaluate your ability to design practical IoT solutions involving real-time location tracking and communication systems.

What the Interviewer Wants to Know:

- Can you outline a clear system design?
- Do you understand the components and data flow involved?
- Can you explain the technologies required?

How to Structure Your Answer:

1. Describe the system goal
2. List the key components needed
3. Explain the workflow: sensing, transmitting, storing, and visualizing data

Sample Answer (Beginner): "I would use a GPS module to find the vehicle's location and connect it to a microcontroller like an ESP32. Then it would send the location over the internet to an app where I can see where the vehicle is."

Sample Answer (Experienced): "To track a vehicle using GPS and IoT, I would:

1. **Install a GPS Module**: Such as NEO-6M, to collect latitude and longitude coordinates.
2. **Microcontroller/Hardware**: Use an ESP32, Raspberry Pi, or GSM module (SIM800L) for connectivity.
3. **Communication**: Send data over cellular (GSM/4G LTE), LoRa, or Wi-Fi networks.
4. **Cloud Integration**: Data is transmitted to a cloud platform like AWS IoT, Azure IoT, or a custom server.
5. **Storage**: Store GPS data points in a cloud database like DynamoDB or Firebase.
6. **Visualization**: Display real-time location using mapping services like Google Maps API or an IoT dashboard.
7. **Security Measures**: Encrypt data transmission (e.g., SSL/TLS) and authenticate devices. Example: A fleet management system where vehicles send their location every 30 seconds for live monitoring, route optimization, and theft prevention."

Beginner Tip: Imagine the GPS like "a digital map that your car shares with you over the internet in real time."

Final Thought: Understanding GPS and IoT integration for vehicle tracking shows you can build systems that combine sensors, connectivity, cloud storage, and user-friendly interfaces for real-world asset management.

Interview Question 98: How Is Data Collected from Remote Sensors?

Why This Question Is Asked: Interviewers want to evaluate if you understand how IoT devices gather data from distant or hard-to-reach locations and reliably transmit it to central systems.

What the Interviewer Wants to Know:

- Can you explain the basic process?
- Do you know the communication technologies used?
- Can you give real-world examples?

How to Structure Your Answer:

1. Explain the basic data collection process
2. List common communication methods
3. Provide examples

Sample Answer (Beginner): "Remote sensors collect data like temperature or pressure. They send the data wirelessly to a main station or to the internet using Wi-Fi, mobile networks, or special low-power signals."

Sample Answer (Experienced): "Data from remote sensors is collected by first measuring environmental parameters (e.g., temperature, humidity, vibration) and then transmitting the readings to a central server or cloud platform. Communication technologies used include:

- **Wi-Fi**: Short-range transmission where available.
- **Cellular (GSM/LTE)**: For wide-area remote connectivity.
- **LPWAN Technologies**: LoRaWAN, NB-IoT for low-power, long-distance communication.
- **Satellite Communication**: For extremely remote areas without terrestrial network access. Collected data is typically transmitted using protocols like MQTT, HTTP, or CoAP and stored for analysis in databases or real-time monitoring dashboards. Example: Remote weather stations sending hourly data via LoRaWAN to a cloud-based monitoring system."

Beginner Tip: Think of remote sensors as "smart messengers that send updates wirelessly even from far away."

Final Thought: Understanding how data is collected from remote sensors shows you can design IoT systems that reliably gather and transmit information even in challenging environments.

Interview Question 99: How Do You Visualize IoT Data?

Why This Question Is Asked: Interviewers want to assess if you understand how to present IoT data in a meaningful way for monitoring, analysis, and decision-making.

What the Interviewer Wants to Know:

- Can you explain data visualization methods?
- Do you know popular tools and platforms?
- Can you give practical examples?

How to Structure Your Answer:

1. Describe why visualization is important
2. List common visualization methods
3. Provide examples of tools and real-world uses

Sample Answer (Beginner): "IoT data can be shown in charts, graphs, or dashboards. It helps people easily see what's happening with their devices. Tools like ThingSpeak or Blynk make it simple."

Sample Answer (Experienced): "IoT data is visualized by transforming raw sensor readings into easy-to-understand graphs, charts, and dashboards. Common visualization methods include:

- **Line Graphs**: To monitor changes over time (e.g., temperature trends).
- **Bar Charts**: For comparing multiple devices or locations.
- **Heatmaps**: For representing environmental data like temperature or humidity across areas.
- **Dashboards**: Real-time, interactive panels that aggregate multiple data sources. Popular tools include Grafana, Power BI, AWS IoT SiteWise Monitor, Google Data Studio, and open-source platforms like ThingsBoard. Example: A smart farm dashboard that shows soil moisture, temperature, and water usage over time to optimize irrigation schedules."

Beginner Tip: Think of visualization as "turning lots of numbers into colorful, simple pictures that tell a story."

Final Thought: Understanding how to visualize IoT data is critical because it helps users quickly grasp insights, detect issues, and make informed decisions based on live or historical device data.

Interview Question 100: What Is an IoT Dashboard?

Why This Question Is Asked: Interviewers want to see if you understand how IoT systems present real-time data and device control interfaces to users.

What the Interviewer Wants to Know:

- Can you define an IoT dashboard?
- Do you understand its main features and purpose?
- Can you give examples of tools and usage?

How to Structure Your Answer:

1. Define an IoT dashboard simply
2. Explain its key functions (data visualization, device control)
3. Provide examples of platforms and real-world usage

Sample Answer (Beginner): "An IoT dashboard is a screen where you can see live information from your devices, like temperature or battery level. You can also use it to turn devices on or off."

Sample Answer (Experienced): "An IoT dashboard is a web or mobile-based graphical interface that displays real-time and historical data from connected IoT devices, allowing users to monitor system performance, analyze trends, and control devices remotely. Dashboards often include charts, gauges, status indicators, and control buttons. Examples of IoT dashboard platforms include Grafana, ThingsBoard, Blynk, and AWS IoT SiteWise Monitor. They are widely used in smart cities, industrial monitoring, agriculture, and smart homes for operational visibility and decision-making."

Beginner Tip: Think of an IoT dashboard as "your device's control room where you can see and manage everything easily."

Final Thought: Understanding IoT dashboards is crucial because they bridge the gap between technical IoT systems and user-friendly management, making it easier to monitor, control, and optimize connected devices.

Interview Question 101: Describe an IoT Project You've Worked On or Could Build

Why This Question Is Asked: Interviewers want to assess your practical experience with IoT systems, your project planning skills, and your understanding of real-world applications.

What the Interviewer Wants to Know:

- Can you describe the project clearly and logically?
- Do you understand the technologies involved?
- Can you explain the project's impact or goals?

How to Structure Your Answer:

1. Briefly describe the project goal
2. List the key components and workflow
3. Highlight the outcome or value

Sample Answer (Beginner): "I would build a smart plant watering system. I would use a soil moisture sensor connected to an ESP32. When the soil gets dry, the ESP32 would turn on a small water pump. The system could also send moisture readings to a mobile app using Wi-Fi."

Sample Answer (Experienced): "One IoT project I worked on was a smart energy monitoring system for homes. We used:

- **Sensors**: Current sensors (ACS712) attached to electrical circuits.
- **Microcontroller**: ESP32 modules for collecting and transmitting data.

- **Cloud Platform**: AWS IoT Core for device management and data ingestion.
- **Storage and Analytics**: Data stored in DynamoDB and visualized with Grafana.
- **Mobile App**: Developed a simple mobile dashboard to show real-time and historical energy consumption. The system helped users identify high-energy-consuming appliances and optimize usage, reducing electricity bills by up to 15% in trial households."

Beginner Tip: Start small — pick a project that solves a simple problem around you, like automating lights or monitoring room temperature.

Final Thought: Being able to describe an IoT project shows you can combine sensors, connectivity, cloud platforms, and user interfaces to solve real-world problems.